The Thirty Five Year Old Secret

❖❖❖

The Karen Woods Story

D1453783

Karen Woods

ISBN 978-1-64003-772-4 (Paperback)
ISBN 978-1-64003-773-1 (Digital)

Covenant Books, Inc.
11661 Hwy 707
Murrells Inlet, SC 29576
www.covenantbooks.com

To all three of my granny babies. Being your Granny has brought love, joy, and laughter into my life. I love you all!

I also dedicate this book to Diane Silman. Without your encouragement and support, I could not have coped with the pain. You helped me when no one else would. Your advice was just what I needed, and I will forever be grateful. Thank you. You are my angel from heaven.

First, I thank my Heavenly Daddy. You are the voice in this book. Thank you for the words You gave me. Without your encouragement and wisdom, this book could not have happened. Thank you for keeping me safe when I went back to some of the worst times in my life. You have given me healing. All the glory belongs to You. I love You!

Second, I am very grateful for Mary Scott, my first editor. You helped me when several people broke their word to me. Thank you for your encouragement and input. You have helped my story be told. You are my angel sent from God.

Barb, you put the extra touch on "my baby" that no one else could. God put you in my life for several reasons. I want you to know this is our book and accomplishment. You "get" me, taking my words, and making them the best they could be. Thank you for being the best editor. You are one of the smartest and caring people I know. I'm glad you're in my life! You truly are my sister!

West Y Market customers: All your support and caring made it easier to go to work. All of you have taken this journey with me. I won't forget the many laughs we had together. I love you all.

To my sweet friend Jada Lane, thank you for the amazing work you did on adding the photo's to the book. I appreciate you to the moon and back.

Thank you Tiffany Ann @ Bradley Wilson Ink for my perfect tattoo. Thank you Dr. Lamoureux, Debra and Debbie for putting me back together, while starting my book.

To all the ladies in my support group on Facebook. You know who you are; I want to give a heartfelt thank you to those of you who helped me through rough time. Your advice and kindness will never be forgotten. You are appreciated by me.

Last but not least, "the sunflower of my life," my daughter Abigale. Your sense of humor helped me through some of the worst days. Your silliness is refreshing. You are my beautiful genius daughter and the best LPN I know. I'm so proud of you. Thank you! I love you!

All of the court evidence is courtesy of Richard E. Roberts Jr., CSR. I appreciate you letting me use your work in my book.

Most of the names in this book have been changed.

For the last four years, I have been busy on this book. When the last word is written, I vow to be a better sister, mother, and granny. I have not spent as much time with my family as I wanted, so I could concentrate on this accomplishment. God put it in my heart to write this, so I listened to His ever-present voice to put the words I feel He wants on these pages. This has been one of those "I can" do things. However, without encouragement from my family and friends, I doubt it would have happened.

CONTENTS

Introduction..9

Chapter 1.   Life-Changing Events 11
Chapter 2.   Exposing the Truth 18
Chapter 3.   The Long Road Back.................................39
Chapter 4.   God: The Perfect Healer...........................52
Chapter 5.   Starting at the Beginning 77
Chapter 6.   The Foster Homes 91
Chapter 7.   A New Life 102
Chapter 8.   Jose..109
Chapter 9.   Acting Out 122
Chapter 10.   James...126
Chapter 11.   Richard "Dick" 131
Chapter 12.   Peter 144
Chapter 13.   Jack 148
Chapter 14.   George..151
Chapter 15.   Four Good Guys (Not All Men Are Bad).............157
Chapter 16.   My Life Today 168

Postscript..181

INTRODUCTION

A LARGE PART OF MY healing process involved researching Willie Roy Jenkins's story and learning the truth about his case. I found three unusual facts. The first, that his was the "oldest cold case in Texas to be solved." The second, that most serial killers are white males; Willie Roy Jenkins is black. And third, the odds of connecting his DNA with Courtney's, the victim, who is now on death row for murder, was 5.7 quadrillion to one.

God put it in my heart about ten years ago to write a book about my experiences dealing with sexual abuse and rape. Though I am no writer by any stretch of the imagination, He told me the morning of my fifty-first birthday that He would give me the words to write. I explain from the beginning what happened as a result of my post-traumatic stress disorder breakdown.

When I talk with victims of sexual abuse, or *any* abuse for that matter, I've found many to be angry with God. Instead of asking "Why me?" victims of abuse need to look outward and ask, "How can I help someone else heal?" Your personal experiences of what seems to be an epidemic in this country can ultimately be used for *God's* glory by reaching outward with support and encouragement. I have written this book with your hurting—and ultimate healing—in mind and to give all of you hope.

The young who are going through this horrible situation, as well as the adults who have not dealt with their past abuse, need those of us who have experienced the same abuse to speak out and let them know we understand the acting out, the guilt, the shame, and feelings of worthlessness. I had not dealt with the abuse I endured until the horrifying secret came to light that I had lived with a serial killer. Then I had no other choice because I had to relive the nightmare I went through when I testified in court. This forced me to take a deeper look at my life. When I started to face the craziness I had brought on myself from not dealing earlier with my abuse, I found that a lot of what I felt and thought now made sense: it had been instilled in me as a young child.

The hardest part for me has been changing my thoughts and actions. I had to learn to trust and then teach myself how to be happy. Laughing was something foreign to me. Now I can get a good deep laugh going over simple things, and it's not fake. That is important to me. I was tired of being a fake. Laughter has brought me out of the darkness of depression. To trust means there has to be truth, and the only truth I've found is the Word of God. You can believe what He says even if it's not what you want to hear. This world doesn't like truth. I see it every day. I have learned to trust in the Lord for everything, simple things, like waking up in the morning, as well as difficult ones, like my health (I pray over my daily vitamins). If you trust Him, He will let you know who you can and cannot trust. And if anybody knows people, it's Him! The joy of living has become a daily part of my life. No matter how great the darkness, God will always bring it into the light. The process of healing, *real* healing, always comes from above.

CHAPTER ONE

❖❖❖   ❖❖❖   ❖❖❖   ❖❖❖

Life-Changing Events

On September 2010, I received an unexpected phone call while at work. It was Corporal Scott Johnson, a detective from San Marcos, Texas Police Department. He wanted to know if I knew Willie Roy Jenkins. I almost growled, "I could've gone the rest of my life without hearing that name!" He laughed at the comment, but I meant it quite seriously. That name I have associated with fear and contempt. He was married to my birth mother. Corporal Johnson explained that DNA had been linked to Willie from a murder that happened in 1975. A young woman had been raped, strangled, and drowned in her San Marcos apartment; she had been just twenty years old.

Corporal Johnson further explained that there would be a trial with a sentencing phase at the end. He wasn't sure when that would be but asked if I would give a written and video statement to the Poplar Bluff Police Department for further review by the prosecution. I agreed and told him I would cooperate any way I could including, if necessary, traveling to San Marcos for the trial.

During our two-and-a-half-hour conversation (while I was still at work with my boss looking at me and knowing something was terribly wrong), he told me that I had not been easy to find. He had spent a week in Poplar Bluff trying to locate a residence for me, but the only one he could find was a previous address. He had spoken with neighbors nearest my last known address. After leaving Missouri and returning to Texas, Corporal Johnson then contacted the neighbors again to find more information on my whereabouts. Through them, he finally found a way to contact me. Those neighbors had given him the name and phone number of my husband, George's, employer. Corporal Johnson then called George, and he gave him the number where I worked.

That set off a minor firestorm. Both the neighbors and George called me at work, wanting to know why a detective from Texas was looking for me, naturally presuming I had done something wrong. I called my neighbor back to let her know it was nothing; I told George in person. I explained in detail the conversation I had had with Corporal Johnson, telling him of the murder that had happened so many years ago and the upcoming trial.

The conversation with Corporal Johnson seemed to last ten hours. He told me of horrors and secrets that Joan, my birth mother, and Willie had hidden from me, then asked me where we had lived and when. I gave him all the places Willie had been stationed while in the Marine Corps, and what grade or age I was at the time. We also partially discussed the abuse I had endured, as well as where and when it had occurred.

But after speaking with Scott Johnson and then finishing my full day of work, the drive back to Naylor exhausted me. So many thoughts went through my mind, I couldn't keep track of them. When he had mentioned Willie's name, my heart sank. How could Joan let this happen? With everything in me, I *knew* she knew the details of this case. Willie had told her of rapes he had committed, and she had relayed the horrible details to me when I was a young child. The thought of her putting me in a situation that she knew was dangerous infuriated me. Now the phrase "Willie is sick," Joan's exact words, made perfect sense to me. How could she take me from the state of Texas where I was safe in foster care and put me in a potentially deadly position? How could she keep this a secret for thirty-five years? If I had known what I know now, I would not have gone back to the house with her, but she kept me in the dark, protecting Willie as she had always done.

Before Corporal Johnson's phone call, I had been comfortable in my own skin, living my life as an apparently normal person. Live music was my passion, and going to concerts was one of my favorite past times. I loved watching the local and big-name bands live. My life seemed to be like everyone else's: I worked, had a home, and spent time with friends. As a very outgoing person, I loved to laugh and be silly.

Less than a week after speaking with Corporal Johnson, I was sitting in front of a video camera giving my recorded testimony and reliving a story I had told no one in thirty years, but that Joan knew to be true. My story was one of terror and abuse by the hands of a man I never wanted to see or hear about again. I began to shake at the thought of having to expose the secret I'd kept for all those years. No one had ever believed it, so I had quit talking about it and had pushed it to the back of my mind while trying to get on with my life. It obviously didn't work.

Mike Elliott was the officer who helped me through the video statement. He asked the questions then just let me tell my story. Since I had known Mike for several years, the process was a little easier on me. The entire interview took over two hours because the camera would stop working periodically. Since he wasn't sure where it had stopped recording, I had to keep repeating myself. When we finally finished, Mike reassured me everything was in his good hands. I gave him my written testimony that had been notarized by the clerk at the sheriff's department, and from there, it went to the San Marcos Police Department. That was the last I heard from anyone in San Marcos until May of 2013.

But then came June 20, 2013, a day that started very unusually. At three-thirty in the morning, my boss called and asked if I could cover for a coworker whose father had had a serious car accident. I agreed even though it was my scheduled day off. I fell back to sleep for a few hours. George had already left for work by the time I got up to start my day.

While preparing for work, I received another phone call, this time from George. He told me that Willie Roy Jenkins was linked, not only to the rape/murder court case I had recently testified in, but also to three other cases of young women who had been raped and murdered. Two of them had occurred in Texas, and the other in North Carolina. All three cases had been reevaluated. George told me he had been following the case on the Internet since he and I had returned from San Marcos, Texas, where the trial had been held. Unfortunately, since we have terrible cell phone service at our home, I lost the connection before we were through talking.

The impact of what my husband told me started me shaking. Though I managed to get ready for work, I cried the whole time, and my stomach was nauseous. During the twenty-five-mile drive to Poplar Bluff, I contacted my daughter's grandmother, whom the whole family calls Grandma. With uncontrollable tears running down my face, I told her what George had just relayed to me about the three young women. Though concerned for me, she couldn't talk because she was at work and had to end the call. I gained no comfort from the brief conversation. I felt lost, *drowning in anguish* and *wanting* someone to understand and *comfort* me.

I managed to work that day and the next two before the constant crying and shaking rendered me barely able to think straight. I just couldn't get the thought out of my mind that I had lived in the same house with a man who had raped and murdered one young woman and was now a suspect in three other cases. The idea that I had been that close to a serial rapist/murderer overwhelmed me. My mind couldn't grasp how I had made it out alive.

I became so self-focused that I didn't care about anybody or anything; I just wanted all the bad feelings I had to go away. The thought of falling over dead didn't faze me. I had panic attacks daily, several times a day, and nightmares kept me up most nights. The knowledge of the murders scared me, and I would have dreams of Willie coming after me again. I was continuously exhausted, and I could not stop the rage I felt toward Willie and Joan. The way I dealt with these feelings (and still do to a certain extent) was to drink alcohol as much as I could so I wouldn't feel anything.

On one of those miserable days, the poem "Footprints in the Sand" came to mind. It was then that I realized God had carried me my entire life! He had protected me from death, from being one of Willie's victims. If He had not been carrying me, I probably would not be here now to tell my story.

God talked with me and made sure I knew He loved me even when it seemed no one else did. Every day, after learning about the four rapes and murders, I would wake up, and with a cheery "good morning!" he would tell me that I would overcome my problems and fears, even though I didn't feel any kind of victory coming. Then a peace would come over me, and I knew I would make it through the day. Not so easily sometimes, but I would make it.

When everyone else avoided me and didn't seem to care, God would always be there—and still is. People are very interested in hearing my story because of the shocking aspect of it, but at the end of the day, it's just me and my Lord. He has always been by my side, a friend who sticks closer than a brother. God has always given me the strength to carry on.

Occasionally, the thought of the trial would come to mind, but I'd brush it off as if it were nothing, just like I had done my entire life, not thinking of the fear and abuse I'd gone through. Once, I was sitting in my friend's house with some of our other friends. One of the guys there told me I thought I was better than everyone else. (I was told he was envious of my present relationship.) This took me by surprise, and I responded angrily at him, yelling "I have to testify in a rape/murder trial!" Everyone in the house looked at me as if I were lying. I knew the day was coming when I would have to expose my secret, and I was terrified.

Missy, an investigator from the Texas Attorney General's office, contacted me about my travel arrangements. She gave me two options. They could fly me to Austin the day before the trial where Missy would pick me up, or I could drive down to San Marcos, and they would pay me fifty-four cents a mile. If I flew, I would not be able to have anyone with me. With all the memories flooding back into my awareness, I wasn't in the right state of mind and didn't feel strong enough to travel by myself. By driving, I could have whoever

I wanted for support. This seemed the better option for me. Missy supported me in my choice. She was very caring and had covered every detail. She further encouraged me by emphasizing that testifying would be very empowering for me and would be something I could do for good for myself as well as for the family of this young woman who lost her life too soon.

For two weeks, I sought someone to make this long trip with me; both family and friends turned me down. I couldn't understand why no one would support me at a time when I truly needed someone to lean on. I felt abandoned by everyone. Even my best friend said she couldn't go. Her reason? A yearly local music festival would be occurring on the day I had to leave. That hurt. Finally, I called George. Though we were separated at the time, when I asked him to ride along with me, he agreed without hesitation. Despite all the troubles we were having in our marriage, he was still the one to step up when I needed him the most.

After finding out the information about Willie from Corporal Johnson, I furiously contacted Joan who had divorced Willie by this time. I sent a text message asking her, "What about murder?" Her response was that the police department was making all this up, trying to come between our family. The police was trying to turn me against her and Izzy, Joan and Willie's daughter. She tried to make the charges seem like there was no truth to them. Joan then told me that they had no evidence to corroborate the charges. I knew this was a lie because of the conversation I had had with Scott Johnson about the DNA evidence.

Joan has always lied to herself and others, making Willie out to be an angel and me out to be a liar. She has torn our family apart with those lies. Who you believe depends on who you are closest to, me or her. This has always made me very angry. This was the mother I had known most of my life, lying for Willie and taking up for him, even though she knew he had done horrible things.

A few weeks before I was to testify, I received a letter from Joan that is now in the hands of the Texas Attorney General's Office. She told me that maybe my childhood memories were off a bit, and that she wished the courts would leave me and my sister, Brenda, out of this trial. She was trying to sound caring and sympathetic, but I didn't believe the words on the page. I could feel the manipulation from the way the words were put. Knowing how she really is, it was not hard to decipher. She denied everything she knew to be true and factual, actually referring to Willie as a womanizer. What a joke! I say, let's not beat around the bush: he's a killer and a rapist, but she knew that. Joan did say she didn't want Brenda and me to have to go through the trial because she thought it would be too much on us. She included that remark in order to save her and Willie, as if we were a threat to them. She was afraid the truth would finally come out, and they couldn't live with that. Later, I would learn that Joan would be testifying for the defense!

I met Lisa, the assistant attorney general, the day before I testified and felt comfortable talking to her. We sat at a small table in the lobby of the hotel George and I were staying at in San Marcos. I began reading from her laptop the testimony I'd sent two years before, reliving each step of the way. When I was finished, she asked me a second time if that was my testimony. I replied, "Yes!"

While speaking with Lisa, I told her I used to sleep with all my stuffed animals around my body when we lived in North Carolina. All together there were about ten animals. She told me that my body knew something was wrong.

Lisa explained the process of her questioning and my written testimony, and that the questioning would go according to the order of the testimony. Lisa explained that I would not have to go into details about the sexual act of rape, just explain what happened at the time of the rapes. I was relieved to hear those words. For the most part, I don't remember the details of the actual rapes themselves. Her last words to me were, "Make sure you get some sleep." The next time I would see her would be in a courtroom with me on the stand.

CHAPTER TWO

◇◇◇　　◇◇◇　　◇◇◇　　◇◇◇

Exposing the Truth

ON JUNE 4, 2013, THE sentencing phase of Willie Roy Jenkins's trial occurred in San Marcos, Texas. He had been indicted on rape and murder charges and found guilty on May 31, 2013. He had raped and murdered "Courtney" on November 24, 1975. I and two other witnesses had been asked to be in the witness room by 8:30 a.m. This was a small room with several chairs and a TV where we met Roya Williamson and Leticia Nino, the victim advocates. Later, we would be moved to an even smaller room with a round table and five chairs just outside the courtroom.

Roya and Leti (as she was affectionately called) were both very attentive to my needs and feelings, helping me deal with my uncontrollable nervousness and fear that caused my shaking. They helped me minimize it by repeatedly telling me to breathe in through my nose and out my mouth. My mouth was so dry, I could hardly swallow; I had to constantly take sips of water. Roya tried to reassure me that it was just my nerves. I apologized several times for making her walk with me to the restroom so much.

While we were sitting in the room near the courtroom, the other two witnesses began talking. I was so nervous I didn't get into the conversation. My focus was on testifying. Both looked at me and could tell I was distraught. The other victim of Willie's was a tall blonde. She told me she wanted to hear my testimony. Her going first would allow her to be in the courtroom while I testified. I don't think she knew who I was until after my testimony.

Because this was such a high-profile case, the judge had issued a gag order for all the victims who were testifying. We were not allowed to be photographed or interviewed by any of the TV and newspaper reporters.

The trial took a lunch break at eleven forty-five, fifteen minutes earlier than planned. The victims' advocates informed me that the judge didn't want to put me on the stand and then have me restart my testimony. My first thought was I'm going to be on the stand for more than forty-five minutes! This also came out of my mouth as I thought it. Leti told me not to worry about it as she tried to calm me down. The lunch break lasted until 12:45 p.m. After waiting for one witness to testify, I took the stand at a little after one. I was called out of the witness room next to the courtroom, and my shaking began again.

It seemed an eternity before I was called to testify. I ended up being on the stand for approximately an hour and fifteen minutes. While I waited, in the small room next to the court room, one of the questions going through my mind was, "Will the jury believe me?" Joan didn't. She blamed me for all three rapes by telling me I had asked for it or that I deserved them. I also began to wonder, "Did this *really* happen to me?" and "After more than thirty-five years, would I remember right?" I'd always been called a liar by Joan. I also wondered, "How will I react to seeing the man who had abused me for so many years?"

At my first sight of the courtroom, I felt overwhelmed by the size of the large space. Walking up the main isle between the two large areas of long benches, I saw to the right of me maybe three people. I noticed the back of Willie's head, close to front of the room. On my left, I saw the friendly faces of George, Letti, Roya, and Misty, along with several other people. To the far left, against the wall, sat the jury members. I had to walk right in front of them to reach the witness stand. In front of me were the judge, the court reporter, and the state's attorneys. Walking up the ramp to the witness stand, I smiled at a female juror. The smile she gave back to me reaffirmed that I was doing the right thing. The kindness in her eyes was comforting. Before sitting down, I was sworn in by the bailiff. I wasn't sure if I was to say "Yes" or "I do," so I covered them both and said "Yes, I do!"

I remember shaking so badly that it was almost impossible to pour myself a paper cup of water, but I managed to fill the cup without spilling anything. My heart was pounding so hard, it felt like it would jump out of my chest. At the first sight of Willie's face after thirty-two years, I recognized the familiar smirk that had always made me uncomfortable. The anger and hatred I felt toward him rose up and permeated my body. I felt no fear, only a greater determination to reveal the knowledge of the evil I had known from him.

Lisa began her examination with simple everyday questions: my age, date of birth, and family members' names. I gave her those of my three siblings and told her Joan was my birth mother. Lisa asked about Izzy and reminded me that she too was my sibling. I responded with a very bitter yeah. I used to consider her my sister, but no longer do. Joan had ruined our relationship with her lies and manipulation. Izzy believes Joan denies situations ever happened that had caused me pain.

Lisa then asked about the events leading up to when my nightmares began. I was about eight years old when I first remember seeing Willie Roy Jenkins. Joan had dated him for a few months before he had moved into the small house in Marion with us. After three weeks, Willie started watching me while Joan worked nights at the Seguin Police Department as a dispatcher. My siblings, Mike, my brother who is seven years older than me, my sister, Brenda, five years older, and Joe, three years older, went to dances and had dates, leaving Willie and me alone on weekends.

Then Lisa asked me to give the details of my first molestation by Willie Roy. I was eight, and it happened on a trip to Seguin to take Joan her lunch. On the twelve-mile drive from Marion in our VW station wagon, Willie Roy asked if I would "come sit in the front seat" with him. I usually sat in the back seat. I was afraid and didn't want to, but he insisted. Doing what I was told, I went to the front seat. He fondled my breast and vagina while I sat in the passenger bucket seat in the front. When he had finished, he became angry and told me to return to the back seat. This was scary for me. It was something I had never experienced.

When we arrived at our destination, I told Joan about the molestation. She called me a liar, as did Willie Roy. I was very confused about the response from them both. Joan had not called me a liar before. Was what he did to me okay? How could I ever tell Joan anything and have her believe me? My trust for her went out the door that very day. Though Willie was fifteen years younger than Joan, he seemed to have taken control over her actions and thoughts, made apparent by the sudden changes in the way Joan talked and turned against her own children, acting as if she didn't care about us anymore. She sent me back home with him, although I pleaded to stay with her. On the way home, I sat in the very back of the station wagon. No one ever spoke another word about the "incident." I don't think my siblings knew anything about what had happened.

Why would I *lie* about a devastating event that happened to me? I knew nothing about sexual contact. The most I had done at eight years old was kiss a boy, and that was the only experience I had had. How could I make something up I didn't understand?

Lisa next asked me about the government project house we lived in, built on a road named FM1044, and what happened while we lived there. Willie Roy had received a scholarship to Southwest Texas University and was the star football player on the Marion team. Joan and I would regularly go to watch his college games, even though I didn't want to go. My other siblings didn't go with us because they didn't like Willie. He wasn't in college very long, maybe six months, before he decided to join the Marine Corps. I think it was because there wasn't enough money coming in, but I'm not sure.

Before marrying Willie, Joan had asked us children if we were okay with it. We didn't answer truthfully since we all knew she'd marry him anyway, no matter how we responded. So we all just said it was okay. Personally, I hated the idea. After seeing how my mom had changed, I didn't want Willie around so we could have our old mother back. My oldest brother Mike had already asked Joan to have Willie leave our house. He did for a few days but returned. Joan's explanation for letting him back in was because he was crying and wanted to stay with her.

Willie Roy joined the Marines and headed off to boot camp. When he returned after three months, he and Joan married. His first assignment was 29 Palms, California. Joan insisted I go with them, although I didn't want to. Lisa asked, "Is it because you were the baby of the family that your mother took you with her?" I answered, "Yes I believe so." I was ten at the time we left Texas and moved to California. It broke my heart to be taken away from my siblings, especially Brenda, my big sister and greatest role model. I believe Joan didn't take the older children because she didn't want any confrontation between the boys and Willie or her. I think Brenda stayed behind because she didn't want to be around Willie. This was just another way Joan showed us we were not important to her.

I will forever remember the day we left. When we were about two miles from the house, I broke down and cried. Being with my sister Brenda was everything to me. Her kind gestures, like teaching me her dance routines for the football halftime shows, or letting me wear her costumes for her performances, encouraged me. She would always show me that she loved me by paying attention to me, whereas Joan never gave me much attention. As a result of our separation, I grew up without her influence in my life, a much better influence than Joan ever was. I didn't miss my brothers as much. Though I loved them dearly (and still do), we were never really close. Because they were several years older, they had always thought of me as a brat and didn't want to spend time with me.

Joan had left the three older kids at the house by themselves. She will tell you that my grandmother—her mother—was supposed to have stayed with them, but she never came. My opinion is Joan never asked her or even told her she was leaving the kids at the house. Grandma loved us children and would have done anything for us. Since my grandmother has since died, the truth can now never be known. At any rate, after being alone in the house for two weeks, the food ran out. The Texas authorities became aware of their situation and removed my sister and brothers from the house, then placed them together in a foster home. At least they had each other.

Our living arrangements at 29 Palms, California, were not the best. The three of us lived in a motel room that had a small kitchen, bathroom, and one room with two beds. It was so hot, Joan would heat up our canned vegetables in the sun! We had no cooking pans or pots until Willie bought Joan an electric skillet. That was heaven to me! We actually had real meals after that when before we had eaten only canned food.

California had dry desert heat, and it would get so hot my feet would make imprints in the asphalt on the road in front of the motel. Because I had lived in Texas my whole life, I was used to heat, though the humidity there was unbearable at times. Because California was so dry, I enjoyed living there, except for the large lizards. One of Joan's friends had a son who knew I was afraid of them, and he would chase me around with the largest lizard he could find just for the fun of it. To this day, I'm still afraid of lizards, even small ones.

I was ten years old while in 29 Palms, in the sixth grade, and attended a school that had both local and military family students. My friends tended to be older and more "mature" than me. I spent most of my time with two local girls, Cindy and Sherry, who were both eleven. They used to come over to the motel and spend the day or sometimes stay overnight, sharing my single bed. Joan, pregnant with Izzy by this time, had recently started working at a doctor's office in town, once again leaving me alone with Willie.

One day when Cindy and Sherri were over, Willie also had a friend over, a man named David, who worked with him on the base and whose wife was Joan's friend. While we girls were talking, Willie picked up his BB gun and shot me in the arm. The impact of the BB left a large painful red spot. He then told me to leave the motel room while Cindy and Sherry stayed. Cindy smiled, but Sherry seemed afraid. They later told me they had had sex with the two men. The defense objected to that statement, saying it was hearsay. The judge sustained it.

Joan always felt distant to me while we lived in California. She and Willie seemed to be at odds most of the time. Once, while Joan and I where alone in the motel room, she told me the details of one of the rapes Willie had told her he had committed. It was about a young woman riding a bicycle through Joshua Tree National Park. When Willie, sitting in his car, saw her, he opened the door so hard it knocked her off the bike. He then pulled her into the car, raped her, then took her out and left her. Joan told this story like she was having an everyday conversation with me. It made me sick. I couldn't believe she would tell me something like that, but even worse, that she had done nothing about it! She never mentioned it again.

A few months after the trial, during my eager search to find the truth, I found out this young woman was Robin Fox. By googling her name, I discovered her story, one that sounded familiar to me. So I sent her an e-mail explaining who I was, and that I had heard her story from Joan. She confirmed it was her and went on to tell me the whole truth about what had happened. She explained the horrible beating she endured from Willie and how she was hospitalized for almost two weeks from the wounds. We have stayed in contact through e-mail and texting. Robin still suffers with problems from the attack. Though she lives in a small town, she will get lost if she wanders too far from her home. She lives with anxiety, depression, and aggression toward black males. I consider Robin to be my sister.

The next woman that we know Willie raped, he murdered.

One of the most painful parts of my testimony was about to begin, and I knew it. Though I had managed somewhat to keep my composure during the beginning of the questioning, the thought of what I was about to reveal caused my shaking to begin again. Retelling these events took me back to those places and times. Though I knew Lisa to be a tough individual, while I was telling an uncomfortable part of my story, she would smile and bring me back to a "good place" whenever the memories became too much for me. She kept reminding me that I was the baby of the family, something I'm very proud of even to this day.

I still remember the looks of unbelief that came over people's faces as I told of the horror I lived through. Sherri, the Hays County district attorney, listened with a look of disgust but smiled whenever we made eye contact. I didn't think anyone believed me, but George told me later that everyone's expressions were like they were watching a movie, totally involved with my story. Most of the time, I kept my focus on Lisa as she asked and I answered her questions. Because she is such a strong woman, she was able to keep her face neutral no matter what I said.

Willie Roy's next station was Camp Lejeune, North Carolina. I was eleven and twelve and in the seventh grade while we lived there. When we first arrived, we lived in a small two-bedroom apartment. I'm not sure how long we lived there, but I remember everything going well while we did. Eventually, though, we moved into base housing. The first night, we visited with the neighbors, a single mom with two children, and a couple, who lived in the duplex attached to ours. However, the next morning, we woke up to learn that the single mom had been murdered by her boyfriend in an alley behind a bar. This shocked all of us, except Willie. It didn't seem to trouble him.

At first, our family life was fairly normal while we lived in the base housing. Most weekends were spent having barbecues with lots of people over. Many were Willie's friends, and they would drink and play cards or dominos. But then, a few months later, I started becoming afraid during the week and having bad dreams, but I didn't know why. One night, I was so frightened by my dreams that I even crawled into bed with Joan and Willie. In the morning, Joan was angry at me because she claimed Willie had snapped my underwear all night, keeping her awake. The defense objected to this as hearsay, and it was sustained. After this incident, Joan had told me that Willie had married her because he was in love with me and wanted me. My eleven-year-old mind couldn't understand why she was telling me this.

I started putting my many stuffed animals all around my body every night. I slept on the top of my bunk bed because that's where I felt the safest. In the mornings, I would wake up without any underwear or pajama bottoms on. Joan told me that Willie Roy was coming into my room at night and "messing with me." I didn't understand what was happening and thought I was in a bad dream. I would stay asleep while Willie would molest me.

The next thing I remember is being barricaded in my room by a very large wooden dresser that Joan would push up against my door. She told me that this was the only way she could keep Willie away from me. In the evening after I did my homework at the kitchen table, she would bring my dinner to my room along with a coffee can (to be used as a toilet) and a roll of toilet paper. Then I would be barricaded in my bedroom until Willie left for work in the morning.

Willie and Joan argued nightly, and though I tried to listen through my bedroom door, I couldn't make out what they were saying. One night, despite the dresser, Willie got into my room. He had tried before, but Joan had always managed to stop him. This time, though, I could hear him pushing the dresser out of the way. I panicked, unsure of how I could escape. Terrified, I went to the window and opened it. It was a wind-out window about three and a half feet from the floor to the bottom of the frame. Since I had always been short, I didn't think I would be able to get out, but I did. To this day, though, I still don't know how.

Michelle, a friend and fellow schoolmate, lived across the street, catty-corner from our duplex. I ran as fast as I could to her door. Her father, also a marine, answered, and he let me in since he could see that I was terrified and shaking badly. He asked what was going on, but before I could answer, Joan and Willie came over. Willie demanded I come back home. Joan, standing right beside him, said there was nothing wrong. Michelle's father asked me if I wanted to go with them, and I answered no! Thankfully, he didn't make me. He also didn't allow either of them to enter his house. He protected me, and I spent my last few days in North Carolina with them.

Lisa then asked if I felt safe at my friend's house. I answered yes, and my voice had an unusual tone to it, sounding almost like a child's, as if I had actually answered from that moment in time. As I heard and answered the question, the thought of not being fearful while sleeping crept into my mind and reminded me that I had not known that sensation of feeling safe while I was sleeping for some time.

A few days later, Joan, Willie, and I went to see a counselor. He told Joan she needed to decide what she was going to do about the situation at home. It didn't take her long: she chose Willie over me. Feeling very rejected and alone, I went back to Michelle's to wait out my departure from North Carolina. Though I was relieved my nightmare was over, I still wanted to be with my mother.

In a few days, I was on a plane headed to San Antonio, Texas. Diane, the girlfriend of my oldest brother, Mike, picked me up from the airport. Joan said she had made living arrangements for me, but she hadn't. Diane asked me if I wanted to see my siblings. I immediately responded, "Yes!" So we drove to Seguin where they were living. It was great to be with them again; I had missed them so much!

After three years of not seeing or hearing from Brenda, our reunion was joyful. My attitude toward our mother had deteriorated as I began to feel a full-on hate for her. I told Brenda that Joan had sent me back to Texas because she wanted me out of the house and had elected to stay with Willie. Brenda sympathized with me, reminding me how much I missed being around her. Unfortunately, our reunion didn't last long. We were soon separated again when I was placed in my first foster home. I had recently turned twelve.

At this point, Lisa questioned me about the foster homes. I told her I'd been in several but didn't stay in any very long. After being kicked out of a home I'd been in for almost two years, the state put me back with Willie and Joan. I hadn't heard from them since I'd left North Carolina. Sometime between my leaving and moving back into their home with them, they had returned to Texas. My caseworker told me I was placed with them because there were no other choices. Though I told her I didn't want to live with them, the state decided it was the best option for me. We had a few weekend visits that went well, so that's where I ended up. I was thirteen years old.

The drive back to Marion took slightly more than an hour, and during that time, Joan repeatedly told me, "Willie is sick!" I just thought he was still raping women on a regular basis, but the tone and urgency in her voice told me that wasn't it. She warned me not to wear shorts or tank tops; that would be "asking for it." I listened to her, but I still wanted to be a teenager.

It didn't take long for all hell to break loose. It would begin with Joan and Willie arguing outside my room after I'd gone to bed. Then later, after Joan and Willie also went to bed, he would get up during the night and start kicking my bedroom door, trying to get in. Since the door to my room was right in front of the back wall of my closet, Joan told me to put the metal bar that was used as a lock for the sliding glass door between my door and the wall. She thought it might keep Willie out long enough for the noise he made to wake her. She could then come and try to stop him.

But if she thought she was protecting me, then I didn't understand. If Willie could kick the door in, how did she think she could keep him out of my room? Plus, the door was so light, whenever he kicked it, the bar just went right through it. Willie was a very powerful person; with his rages, it would have been impossible for her to keep him away from me. Willie never hit Joan, but he would hold her down or back. By the time I moved out, that bedroom door was destroyed.

Once, after he had broken through the door, he stared at me and said triumphantly, "See, I can still get to you!" The look on his face was pure evil, and that frightened me. I spent many sleepless nights in that house because of their arguing and his rage. These incidents were not being reported to authorities. Joan never said anything to anyone to protect Willie so he wouldn't end up back in jail. He had been in prison in Texas and California a few times, not sure of the dates. After the state of Texas gave me back to them, no one ever came and checked on me. They just got rid of me, and I wasn't a priority to them anymore.

During this part of my testimony, I broke down and started crying again. Through my tears, I gave Willie mean glares, with the hatred I had for him obvious on my face. The thought that Joan had always told people that none of this ever happened, even though she had lived through it with me, kept me wanting to continue telling my story. She knew I had been telling the truth but had done nothing to help me or protect me. She had always called me a liar, telling her friends that I had made all this up for attention. Why would I keep telling the same story without any inconsistencies? This attitude toward me has always filled me with rage!

The judge had asked me if I would like to take a few minutes' break. I answered, "No, I'm okay." My only thought was I just want to get this over with. The memories were beginning to be too much for me. I never thought I would have to relive them and especially not in front of strangers. With tears streaming down my face, and the remembered terror making my body shake, I chose to keep going. It was the right thing to do.

I had had my first sexual encounter on my fourteenth birthday with a boy I cared for and had been dating since living with Joan and Willie again. He was sixteen, and we started dating about two weeks before my birthday and continued for a total of three months. We went to the same school, but I had known him from when we had lived in Marion. I was so happy being with him that I told Joan about what we had done (leaving out the details, of course). Telling her had been important to me, though now I can't remember why. She reacted with panic and immediately made an appointment for me to be put on birth control a few days later. I suppose she was concerned I would get pregnant since I had had my first period at the age of twelve at the school in North Carolina. (The school had called her to bring me a clean pair of pants and a pad. Since Joan had never had the "birds and bees" talk with me, I didn't know what was happening to me. It frightened me because I thought I was dying!)

The first rape occurred about three weeks after being placed back with Joan and Willie. Joan had come into my bedroom one night and asked me if I would have sex with Willie. I still thought of her as my mother at that time. While testifying with tears running down my face, I looked up at the ceiling and said "my mom!" with disgust in my voice. I had immediately said *no!* She continued urging me by promising Willie would leave me alone if I would just have sex with him this one time. The thought of it made me feel dirty and sick to my stomach. However, by this time, he had kicked in my bedroom door several times, and terror filled my heart every day I lived with them. Joan continued trying to persuade me, and I finally agreed just to have Willie leave me alone once and for all. I made this decision thinking my nightmare would soon be over and that finally I would have some peace. Little did I know that it would only become worse?

This is the rape that has always filled me with shame. Since I had agreed to it, I felt like I had asked for it. Joan didn't help with how I felt either. She only reinforced the idea that I had agreed to "having sex" with Willie (implying he had not forced himself on me). I had only agreed because I honestly thought he would then leave me alone. Had I known differently, I would never have done *anything* with him.

When Willie finished raping me, I went looking for Joan. I found her sitting on the back porch, crying. Since I had never wanted to hurt my mother, I tried to comfort her, but with no success. She responded by telling me she hated me for sleeping with her husband. Confused by her words, I tried to explain to her that I hadn't wanted to do it, but she just brushed it off and told me to leave her alone. I returned to my room, devastated that the woman who had given birth to me hated me. I cried for most of the night.

The sexual aspect of my life was new to me, and I viewed sex as a monogamous relationship. The only person I wanted to be with was the guy I was dating at the time. Giving my body to just anyone wasn't something I had planned.

The second time Willie raped me occurred when he and I had gone into town together. I was tired of always being out in the country and wanted to hang out with my friends in town. Willie was going in to play dominos at the local bar. I wasn't supposed to return home with him but ended up having to since my plans for spending the night with a friend changed at the last minute. Willie's brother Shorty and I had spent some time together earlier because he was friends with the guy I had been dating (though we had recently broken up). Shorty asked Willie to give him a ride to his house. Shorty and I had been drinking together for a few hours before this. I was fourteen at the time, so when he asked me to sit in the back seat with him, I did. He kept asking me if I would have sex with him, and I said, "Not with Willie in the car!"

When we arrived at Shorty's house, he asked Willie to get out of the car. I don't recall why I even wanted to have sex with Shorty. When I noticed Willie looking in the window, everything stopped between us. It frightened me. Afterward, on the way home, seven miles out of town, Willie told me he didn't want "sloppy seconds." I believe he said it out of anger, and that he was not interested in having sex with me. I felt relieved.

When we came to FM 1044, Willie passed it, then said, "Oh shit! I passed the road!" He turned the car around then stopped in the ditch. Something didn't feel right, and I began to be terrified. I tried to get out, but Willie jumped at me. I managed to open the door, but he pulled me away from it and closed it again. A dark-colored older truck slowed as it passed but didn't stop. The violence of this rape was terrible, with Willie pushing me up against the car door to the slamming on the front seat of his Mercury Marquis. I remember screaming at him, "Are you crazy?" His strength was so overpowering, I felt like a rag doll in his hands. When I realized there was no way to get away from him, I gave up fighting.

Even if I could have gotten away from Willie, there would have been nowhere to run. Only farm fields and railroad tracks surrounded us; no houses, and we were still five miles from the house. I would not have been able to see either since it was dark and late at night.

When we finally did arrive at our house, I jumped out of the car and ran to Joan. With a tear-stained face, I told her what had just happened. Glaring at me with hate in her eyes, she responded, "You asked for it when you went into town with Willie!" And, of course, Willie told her I was lying, and she believed and sided with him, almost as if he had hypnotized her. There was no arguing with either of them, despite my accusations. Taking her husband's side over mine, I once again felt abandoned by the woman who had given birth to me.

I wanted to file rape charges against Willie, but because I was only fourteen at the time, Joan had to sign the rape complaint. She was very reluctant at first, but finally, a few days later, I convinced her to take me to the Sequin Police Department, the county seat of Guadalupe County, where I made out the complaint that she signed. On those charges, Willie was arrested and put in the Guadalupe county jail in Seguin.

While Willie was in jail, he called several times. Two days later, he had been released and was back home; Joan had dropped the charges. When I asked why, she told me it was because Willie didn't want to be in jail. From what I understand now, he was released because she had told the police that I either wasn't going to testify against him or that I had lied about the rape. This didn't make sense to me since it was my idea to file charges on him in the first place! Why would I lie or not testify?

If I thought home life was bad before, it became even worse after this. Willie began kicking in my bedroom door almost every night, then stood in the doorway and glared at me. He terrorized me constantly when sitting in the same room, watching TV or eating dinner at the table. He would look at me with pure evil in his eyes. He seemed to enjoy it with a smirking half-smile on his face, as if he were gloating that he had won the battle. His rages became increasingly worse. Though Joan would stand in front of him to try to keep him out of my room, he would just push her aside.

One evening, he just would not quit hitting and kicking my bedroom door. Willie and Joan's voices became very loud as they argued about me, and I became very frightened. I felt I had to get out of there. After he had once again kicked in my bedroom door, Joan had managed to take him into their bedroom to try to calm him down and talk to him. That's when I saw my chance to escape. I ran to Izzy's room where I woke her to kiss her goodbye, then left through the front door. Though it was late and dark, I ran as fast as I could about two city blocks to a neighbor's house where several times I had watched Elvis movies and eaten popcorn while spending the night with their oldest daughter.

I was running up their long driveway when I saw the headlights of our car speeding toward me. Terrified that Willie would get me before someone opened the door, I yelled and pounded on it as hard as I could. Finally, my friend's dad opened it just in time to let me in before Willie got out of his car. By the time he reached the door, the man had already closed it. Willie pulled the screen door off its hinges then tried to kick in the front door. The man asked if I wanted to go with him. I immediately yelled, "*No!*" So he told Willie through the door that if he kicked it in, he had a gun and would shoot him.

I thought, *Yeah! Shoot him!* Willie had to be warned again before he stopped kicking the door.

The man yelled to his wife to call the sheriff's department. It took them a while to respond, since we lived far out in the country. While we waited, the man had to repeatedly remind Willie that he had a gun (that I think was a shotgun). Joan, on foot, had reached the house by then and told the man through the locked closed door that nothing was going on, and that I was "overreacting."

The sheriff's department officers finally arrived, but because Willie and Joan were outside the house, they heard their story first. They told them that I had simply run away for no reason. However, when they questioned my neighbors, they received a different account. One of the deputies asked me if I would go back to the house with Willie and Joan. I replied with a definite *no!* They convinced Joan and Willie to go home and let me stay at the neighbors. After a few days, though, Joan eventually talked me into returning home. (This incident was not in either my written or trial testimony; I include it here to complete this part of my story.)

I finally got tired of living in daily fear of being tormented by both of Joan and Willie, so I ran away with my best friend Carol. We were both only fourteen, and she just wanted to go with me for the adventure. Carol had taken her father's old farm truck that she'd had lots of practice driving while giving us weekend "joyrides" around the farm. We took off about midnight and headed for San Antonio, where I wanted to be. I had friends and a lot of good memories there from the girls I had lived with at one of my foster homes. They were like sisters to me, and I missed them. I had memories of laughter and kindness toward me, a loving home that was safe.

We were gone two days. While there, I spent time with my friends from the high school I had attended as well as with a few of the girls I'd lived with in the home I had been kicked out of before moving in with Willie and Joan. Only when we started to run out of fuel did we decide to return to Marion, even though we knew we'd be in a lot of trouble. I didn't care though. Just having peace and quiet for a few days made it worth it. Joan was very angry at me, but I told her I didn't care. I was sick of her manipulating ways, and it felt good to have peace for a little while. She looked shocked at my words.

The situation at the house on FM1044 didn't improve as a result of my actions, so it didn't take long for me to decide I had had enough. A preacher in town had children who went to my school, and his daughter and I were friends. After telling her my story, I repeated it to him then asked if I could stay with them. He agreed, and it was wonderful! I went to church with them every Sunday and finally felt safe from Willie. Unfortunately, it was short-lived. Here's why.

Joan would only allow me to have friends from the black community. Though I enjoyed "hanging out" with them, I started drinking again after I broke up with the guy I had been dating. (I had started drinking at the age of twelve while living in the group home in San Antonio.) Despite this, I have good memories of the time spent with them. I actually was able to have some peace from all the rage and intimidation that had become my daily lifestyle. The only one who was allowed to come to the house to visit or stay overnight though was Willie's sister, Sheila. She and I became very close, and the only good friend I had in Marion when I had moved back in with Joan and Willie at the age of thirteen.

The friends that I had had in Marion at eight years old didn't want to have anything to do with me. They thought I had changed into someone they didn't know anymore. Living in the situation I did, I didn't reach out to anyone. Any friends I did have wouldn't be able to come to the house anyway, especially if they were white, so I didn't bother trying to be friendly with them.

I occasionally spent time with both of Willie's sisters at their home in Marion. Jane, his oldest sister, would sometimes take Sheila and me riding around with her and her boyfriend where we'd be singing to the music and laughing in the back seat.

One night, while I was still living with the preacher's family, as we were riding around with Jane's boyfriend driving, he pulled into a convenience store about thirty miles from Marion. Since Sheila and I were having so much fun singing and laughing in the back seat, I didn't notice that Willie, in his car, had pulled up next to us on the driver's side of our car (the side where I was sitting). Then Jane got out to talk to him, and that's when Sheila and I looked at the car next to us and saw Willie. Sheila gasped and looked at me in terror (she was the only person I had confided in about the horror I was living in), but I just smiled at her because I didn't know what was about to happen. I don't think Sheila knew either but had a bad feeling about it. Jane suddenly opened the back door on my side and pulled me out of the car, yelling, "Get out!" as she yanked on my clothes. (Joan told me later that Willie had paid her twenty dollars to do this.) Then she got back in their car, and they quickly drove off.

Terror hit me as I realized my situation. They had deliberately left me with Willie, knowing I would have no other choice than to ride back to Marion with him. Lisa asked me how I knew we were not in Marion. I answered because it had no convenience stores.

Willie asked me if I wanted anything, so I let him buy me a Jolly Rancher apple stick. While I ate it on the long drive back to the house, he explained that he and Joan missed me and wanted me to move back with them. I didn't say anything, just sat there thinking, *There's no way I'll ever move back into the house with you two again!* As we approached the road Willie and Joan lived on, my stomach sank. I wanted to go back to the preacher's house where I was safe. Nothing happened until we were a few feet from their driveway. Then Willie exclaimed, "Oh shit, I missed the driveway!" This sounded way too familiar to me, and I knew what was coming. I panicked and froze. Willie turned down a dirt road about an eighth of a mile down the street and proceeded to rape me. I don't remember much about it other than it was even more violent than the one before. Though it was dark outside, I didn't know what time it was.

Back at their house, I told Joan that Willie had raped me again. And again, they both said I was lying. However, Joan did say she would take me back to town the next day to the preacher's family but that I would have to spend the night there. I took a bath, and Willie kicked in the door just to look at me. That was another sleepless, terrifying night. I couldn't sleep all night waiting for something else to happen, but nothing did.

In the morning, Joan brought me into Marion. On the way, she said she didn't want me at the house, that it was too much for her. I told her again that I didn't *want* to be there. Then I related what Willie had said the previous night about them both missing me and wanting me to move back with them. With a look of disbelief on her face, we agreed that I would not return to their house.

Altogether, I ended up living with Joan and Willie for less than a year. During that time, Joan had called me a slut and a whore and said that I had asked for everything I got. Listening to music was practically forbidden because certain songs would, as Joan put it, make Willie "go crazy." That too was my fault. I couldn't wear the clothes I wanted, especially shorts or tank tops, because they were too provocative for him. It still didn't stop him from harassing me.

A few months after this third rape and without any previous notice, the Texas authorities took me out of the preacher's home and placed me back in foster care. Only this time, I was placed in state schools and disciplinary-type homes. Because of my previous record, no individual family would take me. I remained in these types of homes for less than a year. Then, at fifteen, my father took custody of me until I turned seventeen.

That ended my testimony with Lisa. Then the defense attorney, Mr. Jones, questioned me. He began by asking if my real father had ever molested me. I answered quite truthfully, "No." Then he challenged my account of my flight from North Carolina to San Antonio by suggesting I had actually flown from California to San Antonio. I replied, "The only time I flew into San Antonio was from North Carolina." Then he tried to say Willie was closer to my age, so the incidents weren't really rapes but legal acts. Lisa jumped up and asked me again when my birthday was then, quickly calculating, said, "Willie is nine years older than her." That made the sexual encounter illegal rapes since he would have been over eighteen when they occurred. All during this cross-examination, I could see the sweet faces of Roya and Leti, my advocates, smiling at me.

Lisa finished by asking me how this abuse had affected my life. I answered, "I've struggled with alcoholism my entire life. I've been married five times. I never finish anything I start, and I hate men, especially him," I added, as I glared at Willie. Then the judge excused me off the stand.

As I walked out of the courtroom, I was unable to make eye contact with anyone except my husband, George, who had known nothing of what I had just related except that I had been raped when I was younger. I had never cared to relive the terrorizing details of my life by talking about them with anyone, including him. This sentencing trial, however, had made it necessary. The tears I noticed in his eyes pained me. I grabbed his hand and whispered, "It's over!" then heaved an involuntary sigh of relief. I thought, *Finally, the truth about my life has come out, and people have listened and believed me.* All the years of holding in my secret had finally come to an end.

The judge called a recess, and the courtroom emptied. Out in the hall, the two sisters of Courtney (at that time, Willie's only known rape/murder victim) and her friend introduced themselves to me. With tears flowing, her older sister said, "I admire your courage, and God bless you." I had noticed her crying as I gave my testimony, but I didn't know who she was. I had wondered why she was crying more than me; I understood when she told me who she was. She hugged me very tightly, as if that somehow made things better for her. That made my testifying worth every second I was on that stand.

When I looked around again, I realized George and I were now surrounded by several people: Leti, Roya, Missy, Scott Johnson, Commander Penny Dunn, and the chief of police. They made me feel like a celebrity with all the attention they gave me. Missy spoke what to me were the most important words I had ever heard in my life when she said, "I think more than twelve people believed you!" After all the years I had been called a liar by Joan and Willie, I finally felt vindicated. Then she added, "I loved the mean looks you gave him!"

Missy had told me from the beginning that testifying would be empowering for me. She was right! I was able to tell my side of the story without feeling intimidated or afraid. The courtroom had provided a safe environment for me to relate what Willie and Joan had tried to cover up for almost forty years. Giving the hateful looks let me tell him how much I hated him for all that he had done to me.

I haven't seen Joan in years but would love to show her how much I hate her too.

Lisa walked by and told me, "You did a great job!" Then Leti brought me a glass of water. I turned around to give her a hug and thanked her for the water, but then, as I turned back around, I promptly spilled it down her back. I apologized repeatedly and still feel terrible about it.

A man I hadn't met before came up to me and smiled as he introduced himself. "I'm Scott Johnson." (He had been the one who had called, asking if I knew Willie and what my experiences had been with him.) He said, "I just had to come and hear Karen's testimony!" Smiling broadly, I gave him a big hug. Scott then introduced me to his boss, Penny Dunn. I didn't realize at the time how involved she was with this case. I later read that she had been instrumental in solving it because she would not give up, even when hitting dead-ends or no matches were found for the DNA she submitted. She received a hug as well.

Looking around for George, I saw him talking with the chief of police. I was relieved to be going back home to get on with my life; I felt I had finally done something good with it! God had brought me through a scary situation that had ended with a wonderful feeling of accomplishment.

CHAPTER THREE

⋄⋄⋄　⋄⋄⋄　⋄⋄⋄　⋄⋄⋄

The Long Road Back

AFTER I HAD COMPLETED MY part of Willie's sentencing trial, George and I headed back to Missouri. The trip took two days, and the first day, I didn't say much. Having to think about and relive all my painful memories had taken a toll on me; I was literally emotionally and physically exhausted. When we stopped that first night, I slept like a baby.

George, on the other hand, was very excited about meeting the chief of police and being able to talk with him. He also told me that he had become so angry when he heard the secrets I had kept hidden, that Missy had had to hold onto his shoulder during most of my testimony to keep him calm. I could see in his eyes the hatred he felt toward Willie. I thought of the pistol we had in the car that no one knew about and was suddenly thankful for the security at the courthouse door.

It felt good to see the Missouri state line on the second day; home at last! Though we only had been gone less than a week, it felt like months since we had left. When we were about sixty miles from Doniphan, Missy sent a text message to check on me; she didn't know we had left Texas. I let her know we were almost home. She answered by texting "I didn't get to say goodbye to you!" She had been a rock in my life from the first day I spoke with her. I knew I would miss her, but I just wanted to get on with my life and leave the thoughts of the trial behind.

On the way home, I called my sister Brenda a few times. She told me I wasn't a bad person, and that encouraged me. I have been told most of my life by friends and family, I am in the wrong because I don't love my birth mother. Finally, I felt like someone understood I couldn't love her after the verbal abuse she had put me through. Calling me a whore and saying I deserved everything that had happened to me at the hands of Willie.

Joan had always told me that she and Izzy kept in contact with my siblings, but she wouldn't give me their phone numbers so I could have contact with them too. Joan had also said they all had accepted Izzy into the family as their baby sister. In reality, I found out through conversations with Brenda that she and my oldest brother Mike don't feel this way at all. He doesn't claim her at all, and Brenda told me that *I'm* her only baby sister. I'm not sure how my other brother Joe feels, but I know I was lied to about how Brenda and Mike feel.

I had told Scott Johnson that what I wanted from being involved with the trial was to be back in contact with Brenda. That's exactly what happened. My brother Mike also reached out to me. Both of them told me they hadn't known about all that I had been through with Willie. As far as I'm concerned though, both Willie *and* Joan abused me.

Though George and I had been separated before the trial, when we returned on June 5, I decided to spend some time with him at his three bedroom, two-bath trailer on several acres in Oxly. After a few days, I left and returned to my home in a small one-bedroom cabin on a lot located at Lake Wappapello, about forty-five miles from George's place. I needed some space to try to put what I had just been through into perspective. My whole world had changed when I let the secret out. The few days I spent there were full of rage and drinking. Missy would text me and tell me to seek help. I knew I needed it but didn't know how to get it. My friends at the time didn't know either, so they just stayed away from me. For the most part, they didn't understand the rage I felt or why I felt it. One friend had known my story and knew why I went to Texas but didn't know the extent of the abuse I had been through.

I started staying alone and didn't want anyone around me. People didn't interest me anymore, and I reached a point where I couldn't care less if I ever spoke to anyone again. I did go to my full-time job for a few days, but then, during my days off, I decided to return to George. I needed someone who understood what I had been through, and he was the only one who did. Little did I know, however, that the very next week, my life would drastically change yet again. As a result, I ended up staying with him. Two weeks later, we moved all my things into his trailer.

On June 13, 2013, Missy sent me a text message saying the jury had sentenced Willie to death. "He is on his way to death row right now," she added, then thanked me again for testifying in the case. I cried. I'm not sure if it was from relief or because I was thankful that God had finally taken care of my vengeance. A little of both, I suppose. I hoped that my testimony had had something to do with Willie's sentence. I'd always believed that my day of justice would never come, but it did; the Lord made sure of it.

Finally, I found Diane Silman, a counselor in Doniphan, Missouri, at this time. Missy had sent me the number for the women's shelter in Poplar Bluff. Though they couldn't help me because I was in different county, they gave me the number for Diane, an angel sent by God, who helped me when no one else would—or could. With her encouragement, I went to the emergency room with my daughter, hoping they'd place me in the hospital in order to receive the help I needed. I told the nurse who attended me about the trial I had just been through and the added information I later received about Willie, and she asked my daughter, while I was out of the room taking a drug test, if all I told her was true. She of course said it was. The doctor who examined me what seemed to be a whole ten seconds only told me to quit smoking because my lungs sounded like crap. While he was checking me, he said a counselor would be sent to talk with me, but after four hours in the emergency room, I was released without seeing anyone.

When I returned home in the house George and I were sharing, wondering if I would be able to handle the rage I was feeling, I called Diane and told her what had happened at the ER. She couldn't believe they hadn't helped me; she knew I needed to be on medication. Not yet on the medicine I needed to cope, I didn't know what was happening to me other than I felt different than I had before the trial. After learning of the rest of Willie's victims, I jumped at every sound, started having nightmares and panic attacks, and felt uncontrollable rage. The horrible thoughts of Willie killing innocent women as well as my abuse that had been so long forgotten took over my mind. Every day, sometimes every minute of every day, I was overwhelmed by the fear that welled up inside me at the thought that I had lived in the same house with a serial killer. I was a different person, full of terror, living in the same body.

When I finally actually saw Diane, it didn't take her long to realize I suffered from post-traumatic stress disorder. She relentlessly supported me though my confusion and anger at the way I was feeling by helping me understand the symptoms of PTSD. She gave me handouts that she had printed off the Internet for me to read. When she first mentioned the disorder, I told her, "I thought only military personnel could get this!" Diane replied in her soothingly soft voice, "Rape victims can also get it." Her gentle smile made me realize just how much she understood of what I was going through, and the knowledge she shared with me helped me to understand some of the symptoms I felt. Gradually, the disbelief and denial slowly began to fade.

Within a few days of meeting with Diane, I had the medicine I so desperately needed. She had referred me to Dr. Musser, after the failure at the emergency room, and on my very first visit, he diagnosed PTSD. He prescribed Xanax, Effexor, and Celexa, but I had to drop the Effexor because the side effects made me zombie-like, and all I could do was lie on the couch all day. That was not like me, since I've always had a very active lifestyle.

I had known Dr. Musser and his staff for several years; I had worked with them for a year at one of the Doniphan clinics. I worked as a receptionist for another doctor then moved to posting payments in the insurance department. Dr. Musser's nurse Sharon and I had been friends for several years, while Ginny, the receptionist, always made me laugh with her silliness. All three of these people have been wonderfully supportive of me, even after hearing my story. Sharon told me I'm an amazing woman, even though I don't feel like it most days. (It is my God who is amazing! He shines through me!) Dr. Musser's wisdom and caring attitude toward his patients had always made him my favorite doctor at the clinic, and I trusted him. I would have gone to him by myself, but I didn't realize at the time he was the only doctor in town who didn't require insurance to be seen.

All I wanted was to get better as soon as possible. Despite Diane's gentle help, I still felt like no one understood what I was going through. She suggested I make a scrapbook to help with my healing. I took her advice and went to the local library to find Internet information and pictures of Willie's victims. There were several articles about the Courtney trial, the DNA that had linked Willie to the crime, and the announcement of the other three victims whom the police had suspected he had raped and murdered.

I poured myself into this project with heartfelt sympathy for the young women who had lost their lives. I felt they should be remembered, so I ended up making my project a memorial to them. Just because they died almost forty years ago, they still should not be forgotten, and I wanted to keep them in the spotlight. I discovered that the Courtney case was the oldest cold case in Texas to be solved, so that's what I titled my scrapbook. Though I didn't know it at the time, Willie's trial made history. I educated myself on all the crimes he had committed; Joan had lied so much that finding the truth was important to me.

Most of the articles told about Commander Penny Dunn and Corporal Scott Johnson and how much time they had put into solving this case. Starting in 1997, Commander Dunn resubmitted evidence to the Texas Department of Public Safety crime lab. A partial DNA profile was recovered, but it wasn't enough to make a match. She submitted the evidence again in April 2010, and that time it matched a sample in a national database that had come from Willie Roy Jenkins. At that time, Willie was being held in the Coalinga

State Hospital in Fresno, California, as a violent sexual predator. Commander Dunn and Corporal Johnson went there in August and took a saliva sample from him. On September 15, Commander Dunn learned the sample matched the DNA found on Courtney's body. This is why she and Corporal Johnson are my heroes; they never gave up on this case even though it took seventeen years to find all the necessary evidence. As a result, I was able to tell a story that has haunted me my whole life.

While doing this research, I went on the Wikipedia website to learn the actual definition of a serial killer and the number of victims associated with the label. Their definition read, "A person who has murdered three or more people, in the same manner, over a period of more than a month with a cooling off period between the murders." The FBI's definition is two or more murders. Willie had been suspected—then had it proven—that he had killed four, definitely making him a serial killer.

After a few sessions with Diane Silman, she asked me if I had ever thought of speaking publicly about my experiences. My heart lifted! Could I actually help someone who needed it? This was my heartfelt desire: to tell what I knew so that someone else could benefit from what I went through. "People make movies out of stories like this!" she added. She often encouraged me to send my story to the TV shows that dealt with cold case murders. I did contact two, with no response from either of them.

Several weeks later, Diane made plans for my first speaking engagement in late October at the Eleventh Annual Child Abuse and Domestic Violence Conference in Poplar Bluff, Missouri. I was so excited I could hardly wait. But then, as I started the outline for what I would say, the old question started to arise: would the people believe I had lived through all I had without saying anything about it before? This would be only my second time of publicly revealing the abuse I'd endured, the trial being the first. Old fears started creeping back, and I began to doubt my ability to talk about my life. My sister Brenda encouraged me when she reminded me, "Someone right now is living the life you did."

That was all I needed to hear. I stopped questioning myself because I couldn't bear the thought of some young girl going through the terror I did. I resolved to tell my story. The nervousness was less important to me than the truth coming out. If I could help just one person in the same situation I had been in, that would be good enough for me. This is when I knew I had to start writing this book so I could let other victims know what I went through and survived with the love and patience of a God who never ceases.

During my weekly visits with Diane, I talked about how I struggled with some of the feelings I had. Before I started my scrapbook, I didn't know the truth about when the killings began. I told her I felt guilty about the deaths of these four young women, even going so far as taking responsibility for them. I felt this way because Joan had repeatedly told me that Willie was in love with me, that he had married her to be with me. But because I wouldn't let him have anything to do with me, I thought he was taking out his raging anger on other women, making it my fault.

When I told Diane this, she immediately told me I had gotten used to thinking this way and that it was very wrong. She gave me meditation exercises that ultimately took me back to the Bible so I could begin to think about what my Heavenly Father thought about me. This type of meditation has continually helped me every day with my healing. The Bible is a powerful book, and when you apply what God says about you in His Word, it is always healing. My favorite has always been, "I'm the apple of my Daddy's eye!"

I also wanted to tell my story because of the four victims of Willie Roy Jenkins, even though they lost their lives almost forty years ago. Only two of the cases, Courtney's and Sara's, are considered solved. The police have very strong circumstantial evidence for Nina's and Lilly's cases; that's is how they connected him to those. For almost four decades, their families have had to live with the question of why these beautiful, smart young women had to die such senseless deaths. Some of their relatives have passed away without knowing the answer to that question.

From living with Willie and Joan, I can at least tell those families that their loved ones were the victims of a very evil man, with a wife who could possibly go to her grave never admitting she knew anything about the murders even though I know she did. I saw Willie demonstrate on her what he had done to Nina. (Though no name was mentioned, when I learned how she died and the timing of her death, the similarities convinced me.) I had come out of my room Christmas Day in 1976 after listening to an album I had received, and saw a horrible scene. Willie had his hands around Joan's neck, and I thought he was strangling her. "Don't hurt my mom!" I yelled. Willie glared at me with the same evil I'd seen so many times in his eyes while Joan simply said, "He won't hurt me," with no fear in her voice. While investigating all of Willie's crimes, the articles I read mentioned that he chose to rape his victims first, then strangle them.

Nina, at twenty-three years young, disappeared on December 17, 1976, and was not found until February of 1977 at a construction site in San Antonio. Her dental records and a quilted coat she had been wearing identified her. The timing of the incident between Joan and Willie and Nina's death made me realize later that he was her murderer.

Sara, nineteen, disappeared in May of 1975 from Camp Lejeune, North Carolina, where she was stationed as a Marine. She was classified as a missing person from 1975 until a few years before Courtney's case came to light. Her case has now been linked to Willie and has been closed thanks to the case file being well preserved, enabling the detectives to contact witnesses.

Twenty-nine-year-old Lilly was abducted on April 27, 1977, in San Antonio and was found three days later strangled and raped.

With the knowledge I now have, maybe I could be of some comfort to these families. These women need to be in the spotlight. I believe Willie is responsible for more unsolved murders, with more families waiting for answers. I hope and pray that law enforcement agencies can find those answers, tying him to all the evil he has done and all the pain he's inflicted on so many.

At the beginning of my healing process, no one wanted to come around me, and I would not allow myself to talk about what I was experiencing emotionally or physically. Poor George had heard all he wanted to hear from my testimony in Texas. Keeping all my negative feelings bottled up after the trial took its toll on me. At times, I felt like I would explode. Having Diane Silman to talk to helped me make it through some pretty tough days. She was always there to listen and give me advice, and I'll forever be thankful to her.

When I spoke at the Eleventh Annual Child and Domestic Violence conference on October 29, 2013, I learned that a lot of what I'd gone through wasn't much different from what most people go through when being abused. A few attendees shared their stories of what they had experienced and how they felt about the abuse. They could relate to me, and that's what I needed more than anything since I had felt alone in the world, that no one understood why I felt the way I did. I frequently told Diane that she was the only one who seemed to understand what I went through. Speaking about my experiences helped release some of my feelings. As I talked about that time in my life, my rage, hurt, and fear came out in my voice. Despite all the help I had been receiving from Diane, I still shook when I spoke of my abuse. The shaking is less intense today, but I still do whenever I talk about what I went through. However, releasing those feelings helps me deal with the way I feel, and talking about my past has made it easier to live with my present. I know that I have a God who loves me, who wants the best for me, and who wants me to be the best person I can be.

One young lady, about twenty-five, told me she thought I was amazing. I had never heard that before from a stranger. "I just want to shake your hand," she said. I hugged her with tears in my eyes. I gave another young lady my phone number so she could text me, and she encourages me every week. The reassurance and kind words of the people at the conference gave me the strength to keep moving forward, renewing my desire to do more speaking engagements and finish this book. God knows just what you need and when you need it. He also knows whom He can trust with that task.

I felt like a superstar that day with all the attention and encouragement I received. The coordinators of the conference hadn't realized a reporter from the local newspaper was there, and she quietly followed me around for about a half an hour before she was able to speak with me. This kind young woman, Donna, interviewed me for about an hour and seemed very interested in my story. She did an excellent job of retelling what I had spoken on, although not quite accurately. When the interview was over, I was tired. I had relived my whole story yet again, and my emotions were getting the better of me. I just wanted to go home and be alone. I was exhausted!

But the next day, I was on the front page of our local newspaper. I read the article and found Donna had written an excellent account of what I had said at the conference and during her follow-up interview. She did have a few errors, but overall, it was quite accurate. I felt excited about being in the paper. Whenever I tell my story, it is to give hope to others that they too can make it through whatever they are going through, but you must rely on the Lord for complete healing.

Reliving the abuse I had endured from Willie and Joan caused the pain I felt at the time to resurface. The memories of the nightly routine of trying to secure my bedroom door by putting the bar across it haunted me yet again. I remembered how thoughts of Willie kicking my door had kept me up most nights; and when he did, the threats, the looks of hatred, and his huge body standing in the doorway had frightened me so much I couldn't sleep. During the day, the glares of hatred from both Willie and Joan had been almost constant, with that hatred directed solely at me. Joan had told me she hated me, but Willie, I couldn't understand. I spent most of my weekends in my room. Then during the week, after a terror-filled—and usually sleepless—night, Joan would make sure I was on the school bus the next morning. School had been the only place I felt safe, but because I was so tired, I would sleep through my classes. Despite this, none of the teachers ever asked if I was having problems at home. Did they know and didn't want to get involved? Or did they just not care? At fourteen years old, I felt alone in this terrible situation. I never bothered going to anyone in authority; I knew Joan would get Willie out of whatever happened or lie about it.

My children were very supportive of my appearance at the conference, with my youngest son calling me a strong woman. My oldest son wasn't as enthusiastic about the article that appeared, saying only that "it was all right." My daughter Abigale, my greatest cheerleader, was very proud of me. She is a very strong person with a heart of gold. (Don't ever ask her for her opinion on anything because she'll definitely tell you, usually taking over the conversation!) When she had gone to the emergency room with me, she had cried and told me she was trying to be strong for me but couldn't. Though her tears hurt me terribly, the rage had taken over my heart, and I couldn't cry over her pain.

For my entire life, I've never felt good about myself. I never thought I was pretty enough, skinny enough, smart enough, loving enough, or worthy of anyone else's love. Though I have been told all my life that I *am* pretty and beautiful, when I look in the mirror, all I see is a woman who has grown older. When I was younger, I didn't see beauty at all; I only saw a woman who just wanted to be loved but wasn't good enough for any man to love. I look at pictures of me when I was younger, and I can agree I was beautiful, but I never felt like it. I never could see what others saw.

The men in my life reinforced these negative feelings I had about myself. All my husbands have been abusive in one way or another. Most were more interested in pornography than in having a close personal relationship with me. I couldn't compete with women who were obviously picture-perfect. I believed—and still do—that men want someone who is perfect, except no one *is* perfect. I tell this to myself, but it doesn't help my self-esteem at all. The feelings about myself are not from my heart; they live in my haunted head. I've been very insecure my whole life, and still am. I believe my insecurity is shown by the men I have chosen. The male role models I've had in my life weren't good. Willie is a good example of the type of men I have had around me, except for my father, who was not involved with most of my life. Consequently, I didn't know what a good man looked like. Abigale frequently tells me, "If I put one hundred men in a room and ninety-nine were good guys, you would pick the only one who was a jerk!" This is probably true. My taste in men has never been good. The five times I've married have been disasters. The attraction to four of my husbands had been physical. One wanted to hurt me because I didn't love him. He had threatened to send me back to Joan and Willie's home if I didn't marry him even though he knew that Willie had raped me when I was younger.

What I consider the worst part of my life, though, is that I don't think I was a very good mother, even though my three children have turned out quite well. My addiction to alcohol has almost always been uncontrollable, and God is still working with me about this. I've always put the drinking first in my life, partying being the most important aspect of my day. As a result, I missed out on a lot of my children's younger years. I regret that, not being there for them when they needed me most. Please don't get me wrong, I loved—and still love—my children very much. I just wasn't there for them emotionally or mentally. I didn't know how to love them. Drinking was the only way I knew how to deal with the hurt from the past. My children were taken care of physically, of course, but not emotionally. I didn't know how to be a mother to them.

Because I believed I couldn't do anything, I've always given up on myself and my dreams. My education is a prime example. I was on the dean's list the three semesters I was in college at Chula Vista, California, in 1989, but dropped out after that third semester. Though I was asked to come back, I never did. The drinking had taken over my life by that time.

At times, I have had pure hatred for myself. Along with promiscuity, always having to have a man in my life, drinking, never feeling good enough for anyone, and trying to find my worth from other people, self-hatred is part of the acting out that usually results from the kind of abuse I suffered. Unfortunately, my acting out made my self-hatred worse, especially when it became more obnoxious. The worse I felt about myself, the worse I acted.

Now that I've started to deal with the abuse and secrets, I can better understand why I acted—and sometimes still act—the way I did. Not dealing with it made me someone I didn't want to be. I have always thought of myself as a good person, having a kind heart for others. But like most dysfunctional families, the ones I should have loved the most were the ones I showed that love to the least. I was hateful and verbally abusive to most of my husbands, as well as not showing my children the unconditional love that a mother should. I compounded this by not taking care of them properly, from lack of proper supervision to leaving them with sitters while I went to the bar. Thankfully, though, with God teaching me what true love is all about, the love I have for my children and current husband has been strengthened, and continues to grow stronger every day. I have come to realize that because I never received that unconditional, forgiving love when I was younger, I couldn't really love anyone else the way I should have. You can't give what you don't have. But now, with what I'm learning through God's Word and the encouragement I receive from others, I can give that love.

However, because I'm still haunted by my past, I'm still not back to where I was before that phone call from Corporal Johnson in September 2010, and especially the one from 2013 on June 20. But at least I am finally dealing with the secrets I've kept buried most of my life. Trying *not* to keep them hidden has been hardest for me. You might think that strange, but that's how I dealt with my abuse: I hid it behind people, men, drinking, wild behavior, and keeping a soft outside while having a hard inside. Not knowing how to love, I always tried to live by the adage, "You reap what you sow." Being kind to others and trying to help in any way I could kept me from realizing *I* was the one who needed help. I ran from my thoughts and feelings, hiding them away in the recesses of my mind so I didn't have to feel or think about myself. I even reached a point where I wouldn't even admit I was a terrible teenager living a highly dangerous lifestyle. In my effort to get away from myself, I always wanted to be on the move, never staying in one place for very long, even hitchhiking halfway across Texas. But we all know that our own self is the one person none of us can ever truly get away from.

CHAPTER FOUR

❖❖❖   ❖❖❖   ❖❖❖   ❖❖❖   •

God: The Perfect Healer

FOR MOST OF MY ADULT life, I have had the same recurring dream about a beautiful four-story house that sits on the corner in a small town. But no one wants to go in or live there because this house is very haunted. Anyone who does move in leaves within the first few weeks because the haunting is constant.

The first floor of this house is a very spacious apartment, with a long hallway and large rooms. The entire apartment is painted yellow, my favorite color. I usually just stay in the kitchen because the sun shines in through the large window there, bringing magnificent light into the entire apartment. This room is modestly decorated with a small brown square dining-room table with two chairs occupying one side. Several house plants are growing rapidly on the windowsill. The large kitchen cabinets are made with old glossy white metal, some with glass doors and cleaned to perfection. I once met a woman in this kitchen who was living in the house; she told me she had to move out because of the hauntings.

The second story has beautiful furniture. A plush thick-pillowed velvet couch and love seat with dark-blue upholstery trimmed in tan sit in the main room as you enter this floor. The layout of the space is circular, with four large round floor-to-ceilings pillars of tan stone encircling it with the furniture in the middle. There are three large bedrooms furnished with beds whose covers are old and dirty but neatly made. All the rooms are painted royal blue, with thick dark-blue velvet curtains covering the windows. Because of these curtains, the lighting is very dim. This is the only level of this house I ever tried to stay the night in but couldn't sleep; I became too afraid and had to leave.

The third story is mostly old brown tattered brown furniture, just scattered about the space in no particular order. This area is also circular, with the same tan stone floor-to-ceiling pillars in the same places as the second floor. The lighting is brighter because there are no curtains on the windows. Thick cobwebs fill most of this floor, but thankfully, they have no spiders. The webs are so thick, though, that it is almost impossible to navigate to see what else is there. I tried once but didn't make it very far because of the cobwebs. I've only been here a few times in my dream and don't remember much about it.

The attic contains a lot of old torn and stained boxes piled up to the ceiling, stacked several boxes high and wide, leaving only a long pathway from front to back to walk in. The ceiling is very high, and I often wondered how the boxes were stacked up to it. With only one bright lightbulb to light up this large cold and dark area, it was hard to see where the attic ended. I once surprised a man up there who was very afraid. He told me no one ever came up to this floor unless it was necessary because of the constant haunting activity that occurred there.

I had had this dream several times but didn't understand what it meant. Then one day, after having it yet again, I was talking to the Lord, and He explained it to me. The house is me, and each floor is a part of me. The first floor is my feet; with His "sunshine" in my steps, I've always been able to keep moving on. The second floor is my spirit, the most beautiful part of my being, though haunted and guarded. The third story is my heart. With the many hurts (cobwebs) it has had to endure, it is now hard to reach all of it, making it difficult for me to give and receive love correctly. My mind is the attic. All the bad memories and wrong ways of thinking have made this the most haunted—and the most fear-filled—part of me. The corner the house sits on is the Cornerstone: Jesus Christ.

I've never trusted anyone with my feelings but depended on others to make me happy because I didn't know how to be happy by myself. I'm learning to trust God with everything I face. Before the trial, I would get upset if things weren't going the way I thought they should. Now, though, I have learned to trust God with all situations, whether good or bad. This book is a good example. In the years I have spent writing it, I have hit a lot of walls. But God has told me that it will be done in His timing, not mine. As a result, I have learned to be patient, trusting that writing this book is not only my dream but His as well, and it *will* come to pass.

There are many godly truths that have been pillars in my life. I am an overcomer! Jesus sticks closer to me than a brother (or sister). I'm victorious because of Jesus! I've been a Christian most of my life and have gone to church most of my adult life. When my children were young and living with me, they went too, usually three times a week. I've studied the Bible for almost twenty years before I stopped about five years ago when I struggled with trust. (I didn't understand why I was not getting better emotionally.) But the most important pillar was learning the love of God. Even with all of our imperfections, God still loves us and asks us to do the same with all others, Christians or not. That's how we know we belong to Him, when we are able to love others as He loves us. But because each of us is a work in progress, we must learn to listen to His Spirit within us, being obedient to His directions, whether from His written Word or from His Spirit.

I've often heard people give testimonies about how God moved on their behalf. However, I had never experienced this in my struggle to have a normal life. With all my hidden secrets, I often caused unnecessary pain to myself and those around me by not dealing with the real issue of why I acted the way I did. When those secrets were ultimately revealed, I finally, at the age of fifty-one, started dealing with the dysfunction of my past. In the past, I felt like God had abandoned me or had forgotten what I had gone through—and was still going through. He would let me know He was still with me but would never give me answers to what I needed most. But then He would bless me by giving me joy and a closeness of His presence like I had not known before, even though I still struggled with love, men, money, and marriage.

Within weeks after giving my testimony at Willie's trial, God finally started giving me the answers I so desperately needed, especially about my marriage to George. God couldn't (or wouldn't) deal with my issues until I openly faced my past. In my spirit, I would hear Him telling me what to do—and what *not* to do. The first thing He taught me was not to be controlling, something I didn't understand at first, but gradually, with patience (on both our parts!) and His guidance, I started learning some fundamental lessons of how to relate to my husband.

I learned to let George do what he wants and not to fuss at him, and that God would ultimately judge him and his actions, not me. Controlling someone is not real love. Marriage is a *partnership*, with give-and-take from both the husband and wife, mingled with a lot of self-sacrifice and patience on both their parts. My Heavenly Father kept reminding me that I would need His help to guide me through the rough times in order to have true healing.

I realized forgiveness is the key, and that holding grudges doesn't help anyone, especially yourself. But not only do I have to give forgiveness, I also have to ask for it, sometimes several times. Saying "I'm sorry" was hard for me, but I learned that I'd rather say that than have another person hurt because of what I said or did. Those two little words bring healing, and my love and my marriage have grown since the trial. In addition, George has a much more complete understanding of me and why I act the way I do.

I could not tell my story without giving God all the glory and praise for my survival. The people who don't want to hear about my relationship with Him are usually those who don't want to acknowledge His existence or don't want to believe He will help and interact with anyone who asks. But if I want to be totally truthful about my life, I have to give credit where credit is due. If I truly want to help people, telling this aspect of my life is just as necessary as the rest. Had God not been with me, I don't believe I would be in my right mind now, or possibly, even alive. He has definitely taken care of me every day, whether I was aware of it or not. When no one else was there for me, He was. With all of life's daily happenings, people forget and move on, but God has been a rock I could turn to in a time of need or just for encouragement. He loves me right where I am (though He definitely doesn't want me to stay there!) even when most people judge me because of the mental aspect of my disorder. The PTSD has made me very unsociable, the complete opposite of what I used to be. People who knew me couldn't understand the change in me. The anxiety of being around large crowds changed my social life to zero. PTSD is usually associated with military personnel coming home from war, not rape victims, and I see the disbelief in people's eyes when I talk about having this disorder.

All the healing I've worked through and achieved so far is because of God. And believe me, healing from this kind of damage is usually a struggle, but one well worth it! Take, for example, my panic attacks. They would get so bad I would be paralyzed from the shaking and terror. One day, I felt God suggesting that I try walking to overcome them. Naylor is a small town just a few miles from where we lived at the time, a peaceful town with lots of trees and the perfect place to walk. I tried it, and it worked! Before I started walking, my panic attacks would occur several times a day, with their intensity getting worse. After I started walking, though, my attacks became less severe and occurred only once or twice a week. They have since lessened even more because I have a job and have learned to keep myself busy when not working.

I've always loved puzzles, especially the ones with a thousand pieces. With PTSD, though, I couldn't even concentrate on watching TV, much less a thousand-piece puzzle—or anything else even remotely complex for that matter. After my diagnosis and as part of my healing, Diane Silman (my angel from God) suggested I give puzzles another try since that was something I could do and enjoyed. I decided to take her suggestion.

Before the phone calls and subsequent testimonies that ripped open the Pandora's box of my past and caused the symptoms of my PTSD to come out, I could do a thousand-piece puzzle within three days, usually with just working on it a few hours a day. But after all the resulting trauma I ended up going through, it took me three *months* to complete the first one, working on it three or four hours a day. The second one, however, I completed within three weeks. Now I'm back to being able to put one together in almost three days, usually four or five. It took me six months to reach this point, but it has become one of my favorite quiet-time activities. The Lord and I talk and laugh together while He uses this time to teach me to slow down and look carefully. Doing puzzles has been a great way for me to stay focused on something for more than an hour. I believe God will use what He's teaching me through this for my future good.

If you will only stop and ask—and then listen—your Creator will give you direction for your life. I've learned to say, "Yes, Lord," whenever He asks me to do anything, however large or small it may be. Though He sometimes tells me no to a request, I know it's for my own good. This has been a hard lesson for me to learn since I had become used to getting my way. Consequently, I have always had a problem with authority, including His. When He told me to start walking, it wasn't just to help me with my panic attacks; He knew it would also be good for my health. God constantly tells me I need to be healthy for where He is going to take me. He knows my heart and knows I want to help people deal with the abuse they have gone through. Without Him, though, I *know* that will be impossible!

Finding a good church is crucial, and I've been blessed to be in a very good one for the last twenty years. It has made a huge difference in my healing process. When the truth of God's Word is taught and you apply it to your life, the healing will come. Though my attendance at this church has been sporadic for about half of the time, I always go back. My pastor, now a bishop, teaches God's Word at face value. If you will *read* God's Word, with the intention of learning to understand and not just look at the words, you'll find that scripture will always explain itself through other scripture. Too many people try to interpret the Bible with their own limited understanding and usually without even reading the whole chapter of one book. But the Lord's Word can only be correctly interpreted by the Lord's Spirit.

God will help you to see and understand the lessons from the Bible He wants you to learn. My pastor helped me realize this great truth.

Sometimes the same verse can give you what you need for different situations. Take, for example, John 3:16. It says, "For God *so* loved the world that he gave his only begotten son that whosoever shall believe in him should not perish but have everlasting life." People usually use this verse to lead others to the Lord. But at the beginning of my new course of life, God brought it to mind and showed me that the verse didn't just say He loved the world; it says He *so* loved the world. That little two-letter word makes a huge difference in what God is saying. He loves me so much He sacrificed for *me*, and would have had I (or you!) been the only one who needed it. That's a powerful love! And everyone needs to know that God loves each of us with that powerful love. This is the truth—God's truth— that came to me when I needed it the most.

Throughout all the years I attended this church, I've grown in knowledge and understanding of the Word of God and the truth it contains. However, even when I went regularly, I would be so involved with each of my husbands that I would dismiss the power of the teachings I was receiving. The hurt I felt from the infidelity and bad treatment they gave me would overshadow the truth I needed to know. God is able to show you what needs to be corrected in your life. The bishop and his wife tried to help me by showing me in the Bible how to handle these situations. But then I would stop because it seemed that whenever I did have faith enough to apply what I had learned, the hurt from the problems in that current marriage would only gradually get worse instead of better. It made me think I was doing something wrong or that God didn't love me enough to heal that particular marriage. But now I realize that those marriages were not the best that He had for me. This proved to me that *everything* will work out for our good, no matter what it may look like to us, if we will only put in God's hands.

This truth has finally penetrated my heart, and that knowledge has filled my soul with such peace and comfort—it's hard to describe. When you are resting in God's Spirit and go through a devastating experience, His Word will spring into your mind and give you whatever you need. Years ago, I was so close to my Heavenly Father that I if I breathed out, it seemed that I could feel Him breathe in. But because my faith in Him wavered, making me feel I was no longer important to Him, I walked away from that closeness. Now I miss it terribly. But because I know God still loves me and wants me closer to Him, He's still there, wooing me back even though my lifestyle is not what it should be since drinking is still part of my life. I know it's me who's in the way, but it's hard to let go of my way of coping after so many years. However, with a love that can only come from Him, together with the forgiveness for failures that I need every day, I know I will one day overcome my past. This love and mercy that our Creator has for each of us if we will only ask is hard to understand until you experience it for yourself. And because God is a perfect gentleman, He will wait patiently for you to ask even though that's not where He wants to be. He wants to be in your life and in your heart—always.

I finally found the purpose for my experiences, my life, and it is a flame that will never go out. Discovering my destiny has been life-changing. I now have a reason to believe "I can!" with the help of the Lord. Writing this book is something I never thought I could do, but God has given me the words to express what I need to say. I'm His chosen vessel to help others like me who are experiencing or have experienced devastating abuse. Out of the rubble of my damaged life came my testimony that can help others find their peace and healing. When you go through (or have gone through) a bad time in your life, take God's hand and try to find a way to use it for good, especially good for others.

It won't be easy, though. My own walk with the Lord has been difficult at times. He is the One who gives true wisdom and completeness in any situation, and He expects us to share that knowledge with others. As the Bible says, with wisdom comes responsibility.

Most of my life, I've been afraid of the dark. After I learned of the other murders Willie had committed, I had nightmares almost every night. I would wake up from the frightening dream and ask God to keep me safe. One night, He asked me, "Do you see the stars?" I answered, "Yes, Lord!" "What do you think about them?"

he asked. I said, "They're beautiful!" He then told me, "You are my superstar!" and joy filled my heart. Now when I wake up during the night, I look at the stars and tell God, "You're showing off for me!" In my spirit, I hear Him giggle like a small child.

When the skies are cloudy, though, I tell God, "I can't see the stars!" He simply answers that just because I can't see them doesn't mean they're not there. This was a very valuable lesson for me. The stars on a cloudy night are like God: just because you can't see Him doesn't mean He's not there. Other times, His actions in your life show His "sparkle" so clearly you're totally awed by it. I'm blessed to live in the country, and most nights, there are millions of stars in the sky. Sometimes I just stare at them in amazement, watching them twinkle. When they do, it makes me feel like my Heavenly Father is winking at me, telling me I'm still His "superstar," still His "baby girl." I haven't been afraid of the dark since that first night He spoke to me.

When I say God "speaks" with me, it can be in several different ways. Sometimes He gives me dreams and visions of things that are going to happen. For example, my daughter and I went on a trip, and the night before we left to return home, I had a dream of an eighteen-wheeler whose trucking company logo I saw on the side, sliding on an icy bridge. In my dream, the truck's trailer hit some black ice, and it slid to our side of the road. At the same time, our car slid sideways, and the trailer collided with my daughter's side of the car. All I could hear was screams coming from her. I was shaken by the dream and prayed all day about it. On our way home, we faced the exact same situation, down to the same logo on the truck that I'd seen in my dream. Again, I began to pray for our safety, and we passed the truck with no accident happening. You can only imagine the praise I had for my Heavenly Father.

Another way God speaks to me is verbally, as a thought in my mind that I know isn't mine. In order to hear from God in this way, though, a person has to know at least the fundamentals of His Word because He will never go against what He has said. If you think He's telling you to harm someone, or to go against something that is clearly stated in the Bible, that wouldn't be God. Despite what some people think, He can, and sometimes still does, talk with His people like He did in the Old Testament. Most of the time, He uses this way to comfort me with His calm and gentle voice. It always encourages me and never causes me to be depressed. This is part of my relationship with Him that I enjoy very much.

Sometimes God simply "speaks" through a feeling I get, as when He wants me to help someone or encourage them. I feel an urgency to do things for others. I look at someone, and suddenly I'll feel the need to smile at them or say a kind word to them. I have even felt I had been deliberately put in situations where people spoke negatively about their circumstances, and I needed to speak positively so that they could see that their situation could have a good outcome instead of the bad one they were speaking.

God shows off for us through His creations every single day, but most of us just go through our lives without ever noticing that beauty. I came to realize that most of my healing has come from just enjoying the natural scenery of my daily surroundings: the sight and sound of the flowing river near my home, the trees dancing in the summer wind, the brilliant red and orange colors of the autumn leaves, the beauty created from the foot of snow that we had one winter. Nature is a beautiful gift from our Heavenly Father.

Part of that gift are the two dogs George and I have been blessed to have: Wylie (Mommy) Woods, a female coyote, and Ivan (Poo Head) Woods, a male Australian shepherd/pit bull mix. I find the silliness they show when playing to be hilarious, and every day, the two of them give me joy and laughter.

When we first brought Ivan home at eight weeks old, he was terrified of Wylie. She would try to get close to him, and he would run behind a large trash can that was sitting against our trailer so that Wylie wouldn't be able to get to him. Eventually, however, he grew to the point he could no longer fit behind it. The first time he found that out, he just slammed up against the plastic can. After that day, though, he began to play with Wylie. She was—and still is—a bit mean to Ivan at times, but she is very protective of him. Whenever we tried to scold Ivan for something, she would stand over him to protect him from us with a look of, *You leave him alone!* Of course, now she's no longer able to do that since he's taller than she is.

Wylie also taught Ivan what the straw we put in his house for the winter was for. At first, he was afraid of it and would just stand outside. Then when he saw Wylie jump in the straw we had put in her house and begin pawing it around to make a comfortable bed to lie in, he realized what he was supposed to do. A few minutes later, he was in his house pawing his straw around to make his own comfy bed. Now when we put straw in the dogs' houses, Ivan knows exactly what it's for. For two days, we don't see either of them.

When Ivan was less than a year old, he would flip and flop the ball we had given him (the one he hadn't torn up yet) around the yard. Sometimes when he'd play too rough with it, he'd lose it, and then he'd just stand there, looking sad. My heart would break for the little guy, so I'd just have to get up and help him find it. He is definitely entertaining.

We actually rescued both Wylie and Ivan. A friend of George's left Wylie with us a few days when she was only eight weeks old so he could see whether his wife would let him have her. His wife said no, so we kept her. George got Ivan for me when we returned from Texas after the trial. He was the biggest and healthiest from his litter and has helped heal my heart. Actually, both Ivan *and* Wylie have helped heal my heart. I had recently had to give away another dog I couldn't take care of because I was never home, and was missing him terribly. So while George and I rescued them, they have both "rescued" me from a broken heart.

George and I both call Ivan the "drama king." At eight o'clock in the morning, if he hasn't been fed yet, he will bark and look at the front door. If we ignore him, he'll jump on his house and slide his paws down both sides of the roof as if he were so weak and famished he just couldn't stand up. We find this hilarious! Ivan is a forty-pound baby and is not in the least bit starving, and has the belly to prove it!

If you will look for humor in the things around you, you'll find you don't have to look far. Usually, it's the simple little things that can bring joy to your heart. I love to watch the squirrels in our trees. They are so playful and speed around chasing one another. The hummingbirds are so territorial about the feeder, flying back and forth and running one another off, that it sounds like an airport at times. Be thankful for what you have and thank God for every time He "shows off" for you. If you listen closely, you too can hear Him giggle like a child. It always makes my days better. Being able to laugh and find joy and happiness in the little but important things of life is the beginning of all true healing.

For the better part of my life, I felt I *had* to be with a man. I thought my happiness depended upon this and that if I didn't have a man in my life, I was only half a person. I later realized how much of a lie this was. The few times I had been single, I put God first and focused on Him and what He had to teach me. But when I had a man in my life, married or not, then *he* came first. He became a distraction that drew me away from the Lord and cost me my closeness with Him.

This was a choice that I have regretted. If you are a woman in the situation where you think having a man in your life is more important than a relationship with your Creator, then please reconsider. Thinking this way has been why I've made so many mistakes with men. I was so desperate to be loved by someone that I settled for anyone who would have me, and he would usually be someone less than what I should have—and could have—had. I tried so hard to prove to each of them that I was worth loving that nothing else mattered, not even my relationship with God. I finally realized I chose men who were glad to take advantage of my desperation so they could get from me without having to give much in return. God finally taught me that I am worth much more than my desperation, that I am a precious jewel in His hand. He feels the same about you. Always remember this.

My children have been the ones who have suffered most from this kind of wrong thinking. I only have the Lord God to thank for giving them the love they have for me today. I no longer take advantage of their feelings toward me; keeping my word to them is important to me now. Although there is dysfunction in my family, we are still able to be close to a point and share time together. I love my children very much, and I can now tell them without a doubt that they are the most important people in my life.

Through many tearful, lonely nights, I finally learned that you can't rely on people for anything; we are all human and imperfect. This realization was the beginning of a stronger relationship with my Lord. If you want someone to rely on, turn to your Heavenly Father, who will always be there and will never walk away as people sometimes do. His love is ever present, and I have learned to depend on it. No one can survive the pressure of making another person happy, whether you're the giver or the receiver. Just let others be themselves. Love them and be understanding, not judgmental. An active relationship with God is better than even the best relationship you could have with another human being.

My grandma Acker 1985

From L to R back row Joe, me, my grandpa Acker, and Mike.
Front row Izzy

Our brother Ricky's grave in Houston, Tx

Me on the L, when I was a dancer and, a friend

Grandpa and Grandma Digges

Me, (standing) and my sister Brenda 1996

(Far L to R back row) My Great-Grandfather Jesse Coward, Joan, and Mike
(Front row L to R) Brenda, Joe, Ricky and me 1964

Me when I was pregant with JJ
1980

Me and Abigale
1986

(From L to R back row) Joe, Mike, and ex-brother-in-law.
(From L to R middle row) Me, Joan, and Brenda.
Front row Izzy
1981

Joan, standing, Me, sitting, Izzy on my lap. Taken
at Jeannie Sealy
1979

Me, on the barrel. (The house in the backgrand, is the house I ran to on that terrifying night.) 1971

Me, when I was married to Jose 1981

(From back row) Mike, Brenda, Ricky.
(Middle row) Joe,
Barrier
1963

(From left, back row)
Ricky, Brenda and Joe
Me in the front
1963

Me
1964

(From L to R back row
Mike and Brenda
(From L to R front row)
Joe and me
1967

Me and George the day we got married 2004

Sherri Tibbe
Hays County District Attorney
Courtesy of the office of the Hays Co. DA

Me
Three months

(Back row) Sue (From L to R front row Debbie
and me
1983

(back row) Mi... ...Joan, Brenda, Joe and my dad
Me on Joan's lap
1967

Me
1964

Commander Penny Dunn
My hero
Courtesy of SMPD

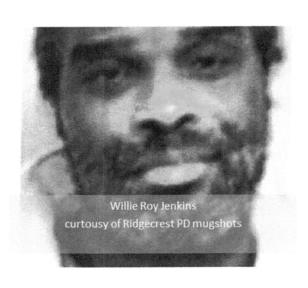

Willie Roy Jenkins
curtousy of Ridgecrest PD mugshots

CHAPTER FIVE

❖❖❖ ❖❖❖ ❖❖❖ ❖❖❖

Starting at the Beginning

On November 20, 1962, I joined the household of Joan and Felix William Billings Jr. My mother was a housewife, and my father was an electrician. My birth made me the youngest of five children: Mike, seven; Brenda, five (my only sister); Joe, three; Ricky, a year and a half but who would die before his fifth birthday due to a hole in his heart; and me, the baby. I don't remember much of our earlier years, only some of the horror stories of our father's excessive drinking and abusive behavior. Felix would repeatedly brutally beat Joan, with all of us children awakened to see the bloody mess he had inflicted on her. Mike and Joe sometimes had to come into the bedroom I shared with Brenda to help keep Joe and me quiet because if our father heard one of us crying, he would get even angrier and come after one of us children to spank us. He was a very violent man. Not surprisingly, by the time I was five, my parents had divorced. Though I was quite young, I definitely remember the beatings my mother endured and the fear I felt.

One night in my fifth year shortly after our mother had left our father and had moved us into a two-story apartment in Houston, Texas, he climbed in through our bathroom window even though it was on the second floor. He then found and proceeded to beat our mother, not caring that his children could hear him in the next room. The phone rang, and we children sneaked downstairs but were too afraid to answer it. But our father did, yelling, "She's busy!" to whomever had called, then hanging up. About fifteen minutes later, the police came and removed him from the apartment. After they left, our mother started yelling at us children, asking why we had not called the police to help her; he had beaten her badly. We later found out one of our mother's friends had called the police after our dad had hung up on her.

I also remember the time when our father showed up very drunk while Aunt Lilly, my mother's older sister, and her family were visiting. The two women hurried us children up to the bathroom and told us to lock the door. Our father followed and tried to get to us, but Aunt Lilly prevented him by standing between him and the bathroom. She was a very large—and feisty—woman, so he finally backed down and went back downstairs. If he had gotten to us, I believe our father would have taken us from our mother.

After we children had left the bathroom, I had gone out to the parking lot behind our apartment to say something to my mother, who was having words with my father. He had taken her ring from her and, after throwing it on the ground, had gotten in the car, trying to run over it. But he didn't see that I was there. Aunt Lilly grabbed me and pulled me to safety. My mother and aunt both yelled at him, "You almost hit the baby!" This made him apologetic, and he left.

When my mother was in high school, she had been in love with a young man named Leroy. However, because her parents did not approve of him (primarily because he had different religious beliefs), she eventually married my father Felix instead. I don't believe that's what she wanted, but without the blessing of my grandparents, she was unable to marry Leroy. Joan was eighteen years old, and my father was twenty when they married. Because both were Catholic, birth control wasn't an option for them. My mother told me that my father had only wanted two children, but within seven years, they had had all five of us in addition to two or three miscarriages. My mother also told me that the beatings started after the birth of Joe, their third child in 1959. Because of her Catholic upbringing, she endured the violence for as long as she could. But within those years, her fourth child, Ricky, died, and she continued to have to live through several beatings from my father's violent, drunken temper. The hard life my father inflicted on her changed her from an innocent young girl into a terrified, lost woman. Burying a child has to be extremely painful for any caring mother, and all the added stress of my father's behavior couldn't have made that loss any easier. Her life had to have been hell by that point.

Ricky gave me some of my fondest memories of my siblings at that time. We were close enough in age that we were both put on the toilet at the same time. Because of that, I became so used to it, that, according to my mother, I wouldn't use the toilet unless Ricky was on it too. He ended up being the one who potty-trained me. I also remember being on a pony with him while we had our picture taken. A man had come through our neighborhood with the pony to take pictures of the kids, and Ricky had refused to have his picture taken unless I was with him. He had on a cowboy hat, and I had a scarf around my neck. Though he was very young, I still cherish the memory of his kindness and love toward me, looking at me with his sparkling big blue eyes and silly grin. I don't remember any violent occurrences when Ricky was alive, although I'm sure there were some. But because he was sick from birth, he received special treatment from my parents. When he died, I remember my older siblings taking turns staying with me in the car while the rest of the family attended his funeral. My parents didn't think it was a good idea for me to see him in the casket since I was only four when he passed away. After more than fifty years, I still miss him and cry when I think about him. He was my protector!

After Ricky's death and before my parents divorced, all three of my older siblings started telling me that my mother had found me with a group of gypsies and could return me if she didn't want me anymore. They would have me do their chores plus mine, and if I didn't cooperate, they would repeat the story. Since I was only five at the time, I believed them and was frightened by what they said because I wanted my mother to keep me. I was the baby and very spoiled by both parents. Between that and this story, I was repeatedly told, I became very clingy to my mother. But one day, I told her the story and asked her if it were true. She frowned and asked, "Who told you that?"

"Mike, Brenda, and Joe," I replied. I don't think they ever got a worse whipping than on that day. The three of them didn't like me for a while, but eventually, they got over it. That was the worst they ever did to me.

Our mother was the one who took care of us through all our bumps, scratches, and illnesses. Our father was always working or out drinking. We kids didn't interact with him much since he usually came home after we were in bed. But our mother was always around. We all went to Catholic school while our parents were still married. I remember my mom sewing my first communion dress; she was especially attentive to us girls. My sister and I both modeled. Brenda was in dance classes, and all of us except our father would go to her recitals. At least, I don't remember our father ever going. We girls also went through etiquette classes. I can't remember how involved my brothers were with outside activities.

When my father passed away in December of 1997, I took a bus from Rochester, Minnesota, to Houston, Texas, to be at his funeral. But because he had asked to be cremated, there wasn't one. Instead, my brother Mike, who had been responsible for the arrangements, took me to find Ricky's grave in the Houston cemetery. But because it had been several years since he had been there, we couldn't locate it. (Mike had moved away from Houston many years before.) We talked of the memories we both still had of him. Mike told me that he and I had been Ricky's favorites, and I remember saying, "He must have seen something special in both of us."

My father had left a handwritten will naming me the beneficiary to everything he owned, mainly furniture, books, movies, and several boxes of dishes. Since I would be going home on the bus, I couldn't very well take it all, so Joe put what I couldn't take or didn't want in storage. I left with all I wanted: my dad's computer and his college graduation ring.

Ricky had been in the hospital several times for operations on his heart. He was in the hospital yet again on the night he died. Our mother had told us how she had been suddenly awakened in her bed and saw a vision of a nurse dressed in white shaking her head no. She knew then that he had died. The terror of that night was still evident in her eyes as she told me this story fourteen years later when I was pregnant with JJ.

When I was younger (before I turned eight, and the abuse started), my mother used to tell me about a dream she had had a week before I was born. It was her favorite because she liked thinking about it and telling it to me. She said she saw me exactly the way I appeared at birth, all the way down to the inch of hair sticking straight in the air, with my face looking the way it did when she first saw me. In the dream, God spoke to her and told her, "This child will be special." I never understood that sentence until recently when I realized God had put me on this earth to live through and then tell about the horrible abuse I would go through.

While we were still living with our father, we spent about one weekend a month with his family. Our cousins on his side were Cindy, Mary, and Butch. (That wasn't his real name, but that's what everyone called him.) Aunt La, their mother and my father's older sister and only sibling, had been married a few times, but the only husband I can recall was Uncle John. (I believe he was her final husband.) He wasn't the father of any of her children but treated them as though they were. If they knew about how my father abused my mother, I never heard them discuss it. I do know my Aunt La liked my mother. My grandfather, whom we called Pappaw (his real name being Felix William Billings Sr.), had been married a few times before he married my grandmother, Nano. Her name was Canis and was my father's mother. My father and Aunt La had different mothers, but they were still close.

I didn't see much of Nano and Pappaw because (I think) they lived far away. Consequently—and also probably because I was not very old—I didn't become close to them. However, when Pappaw passed away, though I was still quite young, I remember his funeral and feeling sad. My father tried to make me touch his body in the casket, but I screamed, and my mother pulled me away, upset by my father's action. When my grandmother Nano died later, we were no longer living with my father, so we didn't go to her funeral. I felt nothing at her passing. By then, our mother had told us children how Nano had mistreated her several times.

I thought that my Aunt La was the coolest! She and her two daughters were very beautiful, and she would always be the life of the party. Her laughter and outgoing personality, mixed with the sweetest disposition, made her my favorite aunt. She passed away several years ago, and I felt very sad even though I hadn't seen her in many years. I still miss her smile. All her children were about the same age as my older siblings. I was always the runt of the bunch, but they still liked to baby me. My cousin Butch passed away before my father did, but I still have contact with my cousin Cindy on Facebook.

After we moved away from my father, we spent a lot more time with Aunt Lilly's family: her husband Uncle Clint and their five children, Shirley, Clint Jr., Sam, Blake, and Paul. The whole family had witnessed the abuse my father had inflicted on my mother. Before we moved, we rarely visited with them because our father was very afraid of Aunt Lilly. Whenever she would get on to him, he would cower down to her, saving my mother from a few beatings. Aunt Lilly was a very large, round, and short lady, and even as a young child, I knew I didn't want to look like her. My siblings learned of this and enjoyed teasing me by telling me I did. Even though it would make me cry, they continued doing this for years.

As far as I know, Aunt Lilly's family always lived in the same house in Katy, Texas. Uncle Clint was always in the bedroom watching TV, never eating a meal with us or interacting with us in any way (I think because he had a bad back). Their house was always dirty with dishes in the sink, the floors not cleaned, and very dusty furniture, and I didn't really like going over there. I liked it better when they came over to our apartment because my mother was a much better housekeeper. However, they did have a yard, so we children would always be outside (weather permitting, of course) playing chase, tether ball, and just getting all of our energy out. Our apartment had no yard, so whenever they visited us, we had to spend most of our time indoors.

These cousins were closer to me in age (something I had never experienced before), and they became some of my closest friends at that time, though Blake and Paul had to first go through a "picking on me" stage. Thankfully, it didn't last very long, and we eventually did become good friends. But then we moved to Marion, Texas, when I was seven and wasn't able to see them as much because of the distance between us. I was eighteen the last time I saw them, but I don't remember where. I just remember that everyone had grown up and had had children of their own, and that JJ, my oldest, had already been born. Aunt Lilly and Uncle Clint have since passed away, and I've lost touch with the rest of my mother's family. It would be nice, though, to see my cousins again, but because of the way I feel about Joan, I've never made any attempt to find them or contact them. I believe my mother has lied to her family about Willie and has not disclosed any of the abuse he and she put me through. She didn't tell my siblings; therefore, I know she hasn't told anyone else. My brothers and sister found out when I sent them the story about me in the local paper.

Joan's parents have now both passed away. Her mother, Lillian Acker, though, was the one grandparent I was closest to. She was a hoot! She had a brand-new tan VW bug that she was very proud of because she bought it herself. She would get behind the wheel of that car and *go*! Then she'd yell "Good Gravy!" at the slightest mistake another driver would make. Sometimes I think she's the reason I have road rage.

Grandma Aker moved to Kerrville, Texas, in the late '60s and lived there until the mid-'80s. I have many fond memories of that house and the beautiful five acres of land that came with it that we youngsters loved to explore. It had a creek that was usually dry unless a good rain came along, and the large rocks would tower over me. With my brothers in the lead, and me and Brenda bringing up the rear, we'd climb a large hill next to the house that looked to me to be the biggest I'd ever seen, giving us all a good workout, and (more importantly for Grandma) wearing us out.

The smell of Grandma's cooking is what I remember best about our visits. She would prepare the most wonderful dishes that only she could make. Her breakfast was the greatest, with eggs (cooked to order), hash browns, pancakes, and bacon/sausage, and of course biscuits and gravy made from scratch. Their delightful aromas would fill the house, making our mouths water as we washed up to eat. Then we'd stuff ourselves to the brim, enjoying every minute of it! Grandma was kind and loved all us grandchildren, showing it often. There were always plenty of kisses and hugs for all four of us. She was the best grandma ever, who loved both her daughter as well as her grandchildren very much. Joan was her baby, and she treated her as such. Grandma and she were very close, though I don't believe she ever knew about my abuse. Joan didn't call to tell me about her death until several months after she had passed, and I now can't recall what year that was. It was very painful, and I cried for several days. To this day, I still love her dearly.

Grandma Acker's father was also an important part of my life. Jesse Coward lived in San Antonio, Texas, until he was one hundred years and six months old. He would gather all the children into his large living room and tell us stories of the old west. We would sit in amazement for hours, listening to his adventures of his younger years. When he was a small boy, Pancho Villa stayed in his family's barn twice while traveling through the territory. "Were you scared?" we would ask. "No," he'd reply. Pancho Villa was a notorious outlaw in the South and was rumored to be very dangerous. Great Grandpa's family didn't think so and were kind enough to give him food, water, and shelter on his long travels.

Great-grandpa's stories of the covered wagons were some of my favorites. He would tell of the treacherous roads and the unstoppable dust clouds that would follow them on their monthly trips into town. He often told us that, as a rancher, his family didn't have much money, but they still had everything they needed. His stories would keep us entertained for hours, and sometimes even the adults would come and listen to him. He was a great storyteller and would let us ask all the questions we wanted. I was only about three at the time, so I only remember a few of the stories, though I do recall sitting on the floor of his living room more than once.

I also remember crawling into his lap. After a while, he would ask me if I knew why he lived on Karen Lane. I'd answer no. Then he would explain that it was because I was his favorite great-grand-daughter, and he chose to live on that street because it was named after me. That always brought a big smile to my face. I think he liked telling me that as much as I liked hearing it.

When I was five, Joan took her four remaining children, left our father, and moved into a two-story apartment on the university campus where she had a job as a receptionist. Then, at about thirty years old, she started dating so many men, I couldn't keep up with them. One was a college basketball star, one an older Hispanic man she took care of in his home because he was bedfast, and then the college guys in the apartment next to us where she would sometimes stay until early morning (afterward showing us pictures of them playing with a gun and holding it to their heads, as well as hers.) I'm sure there were others we never knew about. Our mother started acting wild and drinking on a regular basis when before, she would drink maybe one rum and Coke every six months. She was definitely not the mother we knew. We children received almost no attention. I have seen pictures of me at that time that showed me literally hanging onto Joan while she appeared annoyed with me. The look of desperation, of wanting a hug from my mother and not getting it, showed on my face. She and Izzy (her daughter with Willie) occasionally made fun of me because of that picture.

About a year after we left my father, when I was six, we moved to Marion, Texas, where Joan's dad lived in a small house on an acre of land. The town had a population of about three hundred, and the house sat on the edge of the city limits. I remember the smell of peppermint right outside the kitchen door where he had a peppermint plant. I would eat the leaves, and he would laugh and say, "If it wasn't for you, that plant would be big!" Grandpa had the biggest and best garden around. I'd go out there with him every day and help pick the ripe vegetables. Then I'd sit with him in front of the house by the chain-link fence that went around the property and helped him sell what we had picked the day before. I loved spending time with my grandfather doing something we both loved. This was one of the happier times in my life. I enjoyed the fresh country air and being with my family.

Grandpa remarried, and Emma, his new wife, had a child who lived in Ridgecrest, California. Since both were getting older and could no longer take care of the property, they decided to move there where they lived until they died. I was sad to see him go and missed spending time with him in the garden. When he left, he gave the house to Joan, and we lived there for about two years before moving out to FM1044. Though I did get to see my grandfather a few times before he passed away, our relationship wasn't quite the same without the garden. I couldn't keep it going after he left, being only six, and none of my siblings had any interest in it.

Shortly after grandfather left, my mother started dating Willie Roy Jenkins. I'm not sure how or where they met, only that he started showing up at our house. I was seven at the time, and none of us really wanted him there. He was a very quiet person who wasn't bothered by all of us kids, no matter how loud we got. I remember my oldest brother telling our mother he didn't want him around. He and Willie were close enough in age that he said he felt uncomfortable with that. My mother did kick Willie out once, but he came back after just a few days. When asked why she let him back into the house, her response was, "He was crying and wanted to come back." To me, he just seemed creepy. I would bite him as hard as I could, leaving deep teeth marks in the skin on his arms, then I would laugh and tell him he needed some salt. He would just sit there with no expression on his face, not even of pain. I hated him being in our home. In the late '60s, interracial relationships were taboo, and we were not ready for this to be a part of our lives.

It also had a definite social effect on our family. Because of my mother's decision to date Willie, all our friends stopped coming to our house. I don't even think my mother had any friends except in the black community. I became less popular with everyone, especially the boys I associated with (who were all well-liked by everyone). After my mother decided to have Willie in our lives, these boys wouldn't even associate with me, and even some of my girlfriends weren't as willing to be seen with me in town. In addition, my brother Mike and Willie were close enough in age that they attended Marion high school together; I think Mike hated the thought of having to look at him at school *and* at home.

Marion in the early '70s was a small, quiet town of about three hundred people, so nothing much ever happened. The racial mix was about even with whites, blacks, and Hispanics. For a family of preteens and teenagers, it could be rather dull, though there were a few things that added at least a little excitement to our young lives. We had dances a couple of times a month, bull riding practice on Wednesday nights at the arena located just behind our house, plus the seasonal Friday night football games at Marion high school. Then we'd head to the only restaurant/dance hall in town to enjoy some of the best sweet tea around.

During this time, our mother had recently started working at the Seguin Police Department as a dispatcher. Because she hadn't started dating Willie yet, she had time to spend with us children, including attending the Friday night football games. She didn't have to take us to our activities because Marion was so small, everything was within walking distance from my grandfather's house where we still lived.

My siblings and I were very popular before our mother started dating Willie. Mike was an avid cowboy who rode and trained horses, roped, rode bucking horses, and helped our neighbor get ready for the bull riders on Wednesday nights. He also played football and dated the prettiest girls in Marion. For a while, he even dated the head cheerleader. At Friday night games, whenever I asked her, she would give me permission to do cheers with the other cheerleaders. Brenda joined the pep squad (who would sit in the stands at the games and yell the cheers while the cheerleaders would perform them), the school dance team, and dated all the cute popular boys. Joe, a tough little guy—not tall but very stocky—rode bulls and played football. I participated in school sports as well, especially the track team. Since I was one of the fastest, I attended a lot of track meets. Consequently, we were one of the more popular families in town. My brothers and I actually all dated members of the same family at one time; they dated the daughters while I was the girlfriend of the youngest son.

Third-grade type of girlfriend. That meant eating lunch together and hanging out as friends during recess, along with our other friends.

Along with Mike's other activities, he also played drums in a country band. At sixteen, he was the youngest drummer in the area who could play "Wipe Out." Because of his age, he was not allowed to be in the bars where he played without a parent, so our mother would take us to watch him perform. Brenda and Joe taught me the popular dances: the two-step, three-step, shots(ish), cotton eyes Joe, and the waltz. (This turned out to come in handy later.) I loved it and would go to dances in Marion every once in a while with my sister. All the boys who knew how to dance would ask me to be their partner, and some of them were very cute!

I don't consider myself as having been close to my brothers. They always seemed to have some activity going on. My relationship with my sister Brenda, however, was very different. Even though she was five years older, she always took the time to show that she cared about me. She would let me try on her dance costumes that were all sparkly and cute; I felt like a princess in them. She would also very patiently teach me the dance routines she had learned that week, making the steps easy for me to learn. (My brothers didn't have any patience with me.) Although I'm sure I got on her nerves from time to time, Brenda was always a good sister to me and my greatest inspiration.

After Joan starting dating Willie, my life changed for the worse with a lot of backlash from the black community toward me. Though Willie's middle sister, Sheila, and I became good friends, his older sister Jane and some of the other black girls didn't like me and would call me names like *honky* or *whitey* and would tell me I didn't belong with the black community. Three black boys raped me twice; I was fourteen at the time. Nothing was ever done about either incident, and when I told Joan, she told me I had probably put myself in the situation to be raped. I cried that she would even think so low of me to say that. The idea was that since Joan liked black guys, I should too. The three boys wouldn't leave me alone, even though I didn't want their attention. They resorted to rape because I wouldn't have anything to do with them. I did try to be friends with them, but they wanted more.

Moving to the country from our grandfather's house in town onto FM1044 where we had a brand-new house (built from a government grant) was great for me. I loved living where I had lots of room to run around. There was a barrel on the property that I would lay on its side, then got on it and rolled it with my feet along our dirt and sand driveway that was about fifty-feet long. It was a challenge to get it going, but once I did, I'd roll it up and down the driveway several times. I became really good at it, and it was a great way to use up most of my energy. That house provided a sense of security for me. It was ours, we didn't have to leave it, and no one could make us. Grandpa still owned the house in town. We were all excited to have a brand-new home, which was ours. We had moved so much after leaving our father, I was just glad to finally be settled somewhere. Unfortunately, this childhood dream would be shattered.

My best friend Carol lived about two miles from us on her family's dairy farm. Her brother John and my brother Joe were also good friends. John's and Carol's chores were to milk and feed the cows, so on weekends, we'd ride our bikes down a gravel road to help them. It was fun for us but work for them. We would all get on the tractor and hay trailer to put out hay for the cows. I always enjoyed this the most, riding on the long trailer through the fields with each of us taking turns driving the tractor.

In order to milk the cows, we'd ride their Shetland pony to gather them out of the field. Then we'd jump on the fence that surrounded the corral and shoo them into the barn. Once inside, we'd rinse them off. But on hot summer days, we'd usually end up being wetter than they were, since we just had to spray each other as well as the cows.

Carol and I would ride the Shetland pony bareback together, but since he didn't like both of us on at the same time, he'd usually rear up and throw us off. We rode that horse together more than once despite knowing what could happen. I still have scars from the falls.

During the hot summer months, we would go swimming in their "tank," actually a large pond where the cows would go to drink.

It was deep, so we had a wooden pallet to hold on to. The tank usually had a lot of water moccasins in it that would stick their heads up and watch us. Whenever we saw them, we would scramble out as fast as we could! Carol and I used to walk around this tank, and on one occasion, one of these snakes struck at my leg. (I can still feel it whenever I talk about it.) Thank God, it didn't actually bite me. At first, I wasn't sure what had hit me until we found the water-filled hole it had crawled into. We still weren't sure what it was, but when we finally realized it was a water moccasin that scared us so much—especially since it had come so close to biting me—that we ran all the way back to the house.

Carol was my very first best friend. We got into trouble together, smoked our first cigarettes together, talked boy talk, and could tell each other anything. I've used that friendship to gauge all the other friendships I've had since then. It was great to have someone like her for a friend; we still stay in contact through the Internet.

CHAPTER SIX

❖❖❖   ❖❖❖   ❖❖❖   ❖❖❖

The Foster Homes

MY FIRST FOSTER HOME, WITH Mr. and Mrs. Pullen, was supposed to be permanent. Mr. Pullen worked as a San Antonio police officer, while Mrs. Pullen stayed home and managed the household. (I remember her being a great cook.) Another foster child, Sid, also lived with them and had been there for quite a while before I arrived. He treated me kindly and tried to make me feel welcome. He was sixteen (I was eleven), and I found we had similar interests, primarily in music and food. Our favorite singer was Elton John, and some nights after we finished our homework and chores, we'd just sit and listen to his albums. The school we attended was across the street from the house. I can't recall anything else about it other than that.

After I'd been there about three months, I borrowed a T-shirt from Sid that had a concert advertised on it. I don't remember the name of the band other than there was a picture of the band on the front and concert dates on the back. With me being small at the time, the T-shirt was oversized for me. Mrs. Pullen didn't want me leaving the house dressed that way, so she pulled me up the stairs by my arm (rather roughly, I thought) and made me put on a more feminine-looking shirt. For some reason, she didn't want me wearing T-shirts, although I was allowed to wear jeans. She must have called

Child Welfare and asked that I be placed somewhere else because shortly after this incident, I was taken out of this home. I hadn't been there long enough for this to upset me, although I did miss Sid.

My second foster home was supposed to be a thirty-day temporary group home, but I ended up staying for two months because the state couldn't find anywhere more permanent for me. The foster parents were great! They were essentially big kids themselves, so they were easy to talk to with lighthearted conversations. Around the dinner table, we'd just laugh and joke with each other. No one attended school here, so we had a lot of outings to the zoo, the parks, and the local swimming pool. I knew I wouldn't be there long, so I tried not to become too attached to any of the other girls. But I did anyway even though most of them came and went while I was there. I remember one very well because she had taken several yellow jackets (a form of speed in a black-and-yellow pill) and started slipping in and out of consciousness. We all piled into the van and rushed her to the emergency room. Thankfully, she survived.

From there, I went to my third foster home where I stayed about a year and a half, the longest I stayed in any of the homes I was placed. The Buckner Baptist Benevolence Home for Girls in San Antonio, Texas, was a group home for unwed pregnant girls and wards of the state. It was like having thirty sisters since we interacted with each other as one big family. The unwed mothers had a different housing area than the wards of the state, but we all ate in the same dining area. I went through my eighth and part of my ninth years of school there. Our house mothers, Susan, Ava, and Brenda, were greathearted women who made good role models for all of us. At one time, there were seven of us living in the house for the wards of the state, the maximum number allowed. Usually, we girls would all get along, but occasionally, there would be a few who would start a fight over anything. Since this was a permanent home, finding another foster home for someone who didn't get along with the other girls was almost impossible. One young lady named Julie always seemed to get on the bad side of another girl, causing many fights between them. This other girl was the "leader" of the house and would get angry at the rest of us if we interacted with Julie. Consequently, she mostly stayed by herself. I liked her though, and when I married for the first time, she was one of my witnesses.

Time at Buckner was not without tragedy, however. After I had been there about a year, Brenda (one of our house mothers) committed suicide with her dog Josie. She drove her car into the garage at her residence and let it run with a hose from the exhaust placed inside the vehicle. They found her and Josie the next day. We were not told if there was a note or any reason for her killing herself and her dog. Everyone in our house was devastated; with broken hearts, we tried to comfort each other. At the funeral in Lubbock, Brenda's family called us "Brenda's Girls" because she had talked often about us, telling them how much she enjoyed working with us. We were her life, she had told them, and dearly loved all of us. The feeling was mutual, and her death left an empty spot in each of our lives.

One very good thing did happen while I was there, though: before Brenda died, I accepted Jesus Christ as my Lord and Savior and was later baptized. One of the sermons given at the First Baptist Church that we attended in San Antonio caught my attention. The preacher spoke about heaven and hell, what these places looked like, and where we would spend our eternity. After he finished and the invitation to turn our lives over to the Lord was given, I practically floated down the aisle to the altar. A few weeks later, I was baptized at an evening service. As I was brought out of the water, I felt as clean as I had ever been in my life, thoroughly clean, inside and out, and oh, it felt so good! It was an amazing feeling, one that I've never felt since. My happiness must have been obvious—I know I had a huge smile on my face—because as I stood there, dripping wet, I looked at the congregation, and they shared my joy with their own smiles and laughter. That gave me a sense of belonging, of being welcome just as I was, that made me even happier. I knew this experience would change my life, and it did. But unfortunately, not until ten years later.

When I arrived at Buckner, I experienced a lot of firsts. I had my first boyfriend, first real kiss, first (boyfriend) heartbreak, and drank alcohol and used illegal drugs for the first time. This all, of course, had to be done secretly, with a lot of nighttime sneaking through windows while the house mothers slept. We were teenagers and so wanted to do what most other teenagers were doing to be part of the crowd. It being the '70s, when alcohol, illegal drug use, loud music and contempt for authority were on the rise, this usually meant that's what the crowd did, and I went along just to be accepted (how I've coped with my feelings most of my life).

The alcohol and drug use came from the parties we went to. At first, I did it just to go along with everyone else, but then I started enjoying it and wanted more. My boyfriend, Jeff (who gave me my first kiss), with his best friend and his girlfriend from the home, would ride around in his beautiful blue Mustang and listen to Thin Lizzy. At eighteen, he was stabbed to death in his car outside a restaurant in San Antonio. Thankfully, they arrested the guy who killed him. When Jeff's friend called to tell me he had been killed, I was heartbroken. I still think of him whenever I hear Thin Lizzy's music.

With all this sneaking around, we were bound to get caught. One night, Denise and I had gotten so drunk that when we climbed back in through the window, I fell back into the window and onto the toilet and made too much noise. It woke Susan, one of our house mothers, and she investigated. The other girl had made it to her bed and was covered, so I was the only one Susan caught. (I didn't say anything about Denise.) Needless to say, she was very angry with me. In the morning, she told me that the rest of the staff would have to be told, and then they would have to review my situation. A few days later, I received the bad news: I had to be removed from the home and returned to Joan and Willie.

My nightmare had come true. I had never wanted to live with Joan and Willie again. Remembering the abuse he had put me through terrified me. Knowing what I knew about him, I didn't think he had changed. I was very happy at Buckner's and didn't want to leave; they were truly my family. Denise and I were roommates; our room was on the bottom floor of the two-story house, and that's what had made it easy for us to sneak in and out. A few of the other girls would go with us sometimes, but for the most part, it was just her and me. I have regretted doing it since that day.

After almost a year of supposedly being in the care of Joan and Willie, not one person from the welfare office came by to check on me. It was during this time that I had started living with the preacher's family in Marion. Eventually though, the child welfare office learned about it, and because it wasn't a state-approved arrangement, they immediately removed me. They temporarily placed me in an approved home with the McCormick's, who had two daughters, Sheri and Lori, and a son whose name I don't recall.

While living there, I shared Lori's bedroom. I had always been afraid of the dark, and the nightmares I had of Willie coming after me didn't help any. The terror he had inflicted on my soul wouldn't leave me, making me unable to feel safe anywhere. Unable to sleep, I would sit up in my bed and tell her how frightened I was. Panic would overcome me, and Lori always tried to comfort me by telling me, "You're safe" or "It's okay." Sometimes she would stay up with me so I wouldn't have to be awake alone. She treated me very kindly and tried to help me feel safe and comfortable in her home. She was the sister I so desperately needed; I missed my real sister less because of her.

Though I don't remember much about Mr. McCormick, I do remember his wife didn't know how to deal with me. Looking back, I think she never had to deal with a foster child who had as many psychological problems as I did. She didn't have the patience with me that Lori had. She would tell me to go to bed, but I'd cry and tell her I was afraid to go to sleep. Though I was fourteen at the time, I did this just about every night, and I'm sure it wore on her nerves. Not to mention the anxiety I felt whenever bedtime approached. Mrs. McCormick wasn't mean to me, but instead of trying to comfort me as Lori did, she would speak sternly to me. One night, Mr. McCormick took my side when his wife tried to get me to bed. I don't remember what he said, but she eventually just walked away while I stayed up late watching TV in the living room. They eventually put a night-light in the room that did help; it was bright enough I could see everything if I woke up. Sometimes, that light was the only comfort I'd have when everyone else was asleep.

The McCormick's managed some regional Dairy Queens, giving me a part-time job at the Seguin location with the benefit of free food. I loved it! In addition, I'd sometimes travel with them to check on their other stores. Since they were in different cities, some of the trips were quite long, so we made them fun by singing songs and laughing at jokes. These people were the closest thing to a real family I had had in a long time. I felt comfortable with them, like I belonged, even being included in family time. The feeling must have been mutual because eventually, everyone in the family showed me love and comforted me whenever I was in distress. Unfortunately, theirs was not a permanent home (a temporary home was usually thirty days, but I stayed sixty days, I believe), and I ended up being moved yet again. I found this painful and missed them terribly.

The next (and thankfully, last) two foster "homes" were not like the ones I had been in before. They were group homes that treated us foster children very rough, and each of them had a greater number of girls. The first had all girls whose ages ranged from four to seventeen, while the second had a mixture of girls and boys, the youngest being nine and the oldest seventeen. They were classified as state schools, and I didn't like either one. I was very glad when I was able to leave both of them.

The first one was in Henderson, in the east part of Texas. I had been raised in Central Texas where the beautiful scenery had rivers, hills, and a mixture of trees with many great camping spots. Eastern Texas, however, had red clay with some hills and only pine trees and was hotter and more humid than what I was used to. I hated it there and ran away as often as I could, not just because of the environment, but also because I didn't want to become like the other girls who had been in foster homes so long, they were now part of the system. They usually chose to deal with their problems by fighting instead of talking about them with someone. Many of them were bigger than me and would often choose to take their anger and frustrations out on me. I'd run away to get away from the fighting and verbal abuse. By this time, at the age of fifteen, any confrontation frightened me, and I had become very timid in the face of aggression. Consequently, I became a "doormat," letting other people walk all over me. Because I didn't know how to defend myself, I'd run away. I found that to be easier than trying to deal with the overpowering dominance of another person.

The large house we lived in was managed like a very large family except with fifteen girls living there, it was no family. Everyone had chores, and we would eat around two very long tables. This is also where we did our homework from the public school we attended.

Punishment for any infraction of the rules—but especially for running away—was harsh. With our hands behind us, we had to stand about a foot from the wall while holding a large city phone book against it with our noses. We were made to do this for at least three hours, what most of the other girls had to do. But for me, the shortest time was four hours, and the longest six.

Four times I escaped and was caught, and three times I had to hold the stupid phone book against the wall with my nose. At least two other girls would always go with me, and they would have to endure this painful punishment as well. I always felt terrible for them since it was my idea to leave. The house parents began sealing the windows so I couldn't get out, but I always found a way. They began calling me "the mastermind." After my fourth escape, though, they had finally had enough, saying I was too much of a liability. They left me in jail instead of getting me out, and I stayed there until the state could find a way to deal with me. By this time, all the permanent group homes had had their fill of me. Everyone had had their fill of me, and so I ended up being sent to yet another state school.

Running away from this group home was not without its dangers. The first time I ran away, two other girls went with me, and we were living in an apartment in the Seguin area. One night, I answered a knock on the door, and two black men with knives barged in. We had no idea who they were or how they knew we were there. They warned us that the first girl to leave the living room of the apartment would be raped. I chose to be that first girl to protect the others, so I went to the kitchen to get a glass of water. That's when one of them pulled his knife on me and held it to my throat. They told the others to leave the apartment, but Jennifer didn't want to. Jennifer, another girl, and I and the two black guys sat in the apartment about two hours before they raped me. I just wanted them to leave. Before they left, they threatened all of us that if we told on them, they would come back and kill us.

Another time I ran away, I had a pistol pointed at me by an older man who wanted to have sex, but I refused. I had been hanging out at a small bar, had become friends with some of the older men, and had started playing pool with them. I guess the one with the gun thought I was teasing him, but when he realized I wasn't, he became angry at me. At this same time and unknown to me, the twenty-one-year-old guy I was living with had been planning to sell me into slavery. The police told me this after I had been found and arrested.

Jennifer, who I thought of as my foster sister, always went with me when I ran away, with usually at least two other girls leaving with us (though not the same ones). We'd be gone anywhere from six weeks to two months before we were found and returned to the home. Jennifer and I were usually the last ones caught because we'd separate ourselves from the others, then watch them from a distance to determine what they were doing to bring the attention of the police to them. We learned from these experiences and figured out what *not* to do.

After being arrested and waiting for someone to bail us out of the Seguin city jail, two of the officers would bring us candy and then have sex with us in our jail cell. The sex was always voluntary, and no one ever found out. But after being in jail a few weeks, the boredom became too much, so we'd invent ways to amuse ourselves. One time, Jennifer and I shoved rolls of toilet paper down the toilet to clog it and flood the cell so we could go "swimming" in the whole two inches of water that accumulated. I had a lot of anger in me so I didn't care that I was destroying someone else's property. Three years later, Joan told me that we did over twenty-thousand dollars' worth of damage to that jail. I laughed. It felt good to hurt someone. I no longer find it funny and feel ashamed of myself.

We eventually were sent back to the foster home and again was punished in the same way. The next time I ran away was the last time. I don't remember much about that time of running away except I was in a very small town when Jennifer and I were caught. The jail cell we were placed in was opened to the outside, and the trustees would bring us marijuana and talk to us all day. The foster home would no longer take me back. Jennifer, on the other hand, was returned to the home within days of us getting caught. I remained in jail until the state of Texas found a state school to put me in.

At this time in my life, I didn't care about myself; I just wanted to stop hurting, and sex was one of the ways I coped with it. I was a mess of a person. This is what I refer to as acting out. The more I hurt, the more I would make bad decisions—like having sex with just anyone—leading to more hurt, lack of self-esteem, and regret.

The next—and last—"home" where Child Welfare placed me was another state school. This one was located in Austin, Texas. Daily activities like school, eating, sleeping, and free time were very structured. Every meal was served at a certain time each day, and if you missed it, there was no food until the next one. School classes and meals were a mixture of boys and girls, but each had their own dorm, with the boys' dorm being larger. This "home" was point-based, meaning a person had to have so many points—1,200 I think—in order to be released. These were given for doing what was required (chores, schoolwork, keeping your room clean, and passing the daily room check) and *not* getting into trouble. If we did anything wrong, even little things like being late for where we were supposed to be, or not doing our homework, points would be taken away.

Despite the strictness of the rules, this was still one rough place, and I was very much an outsider. These kids weren't just wards of the state but also had had trouble with the law. In fact, most were there for committing crimes like robbery and assault. There was one other white person, a boy, and the other two races, blacks and Hispanics, ran in their own groups. I'd immerse myself in my school studies just to stay away from everyone, even staff, and most of my days were spent alone. When I first arrived, my roommate was a black girl, who was very friendly to me. After being there about a month though, the other girls in our hall convinced her to unfriend me. I tried to speak to the others, but they ignored me. The only conversations I had were with our teachers, and then only about schoolwork. I was there about five months. Thankfully, my father had found me shortly after I had arrived, so I had someplace to go when I was released. After finding out I would be released to my father and stepmother, I worked even harder to get out. I knew there would be no more foster homes for me, and that they would take care of me!

Shortly after arriving at the state school, the supervisor of the Child Welfare office, Mrs. Dalton, had contacted my father and asked him to come to her office in Seguin where she shared my file with him and my stepmother. Dad later told me my file was so thick it had its own filing cabinet drawer. He learned of all the foster homes I'd been in and the four times I had run away. He also learned I had been sent back to live with Joan and Willie. My father didn't know of any of the abuse I had endured from them both since he hadn't been in my life since I was five. Now, at the age of fifteen, he was ready to take me home. All he could say to Mrs. Dalton was, "She just wants to be loved."

Four girls at this school, three black and one Hispanic, didn't like me for some reason. They would find any excuse (and sometimes no excuse) to pick on and harass me. They started doing this after I'd been there about a month. After about two months, these girls wrote "Ava is a bitch" on the door of one of the stalls in the bathroom in our hall, then blamed me for it. (Ava was the Hispanic girl.) The staff told me to write the same words on a piece of paper to see if the handwriting matched. Of course, it didn't. After that, the girls left me alone for a few weeks.

But then a few days before I was to be released, two of these girls caught me having sex with one of the male staff members. He had started being kind to me about a week before, finally giving me someone to talk to. (And no, this was not acceptable behavior for the staff, but I believe it was a regular occurrence there. Thankfully, all the girls were put on birth control when they first arrived.) Anyway, one of the girls became furious and let me know in no uncertain terms that that staff member was also having sex with her, and because she had been there longer, he was *hers*, and I was not to have anything to do with him anymore. Later, all four of these girls barged into my bedroom at night and beat me up. I ended up with a black eye and several bruises. If any of the staff noticed, nothing was said to me. They all knew I wouldn't tell them what had happened anyway. When my father came to get me and saw the results of their beating, he was furious and wanted to report them. I told him not to; I was just relieved to be leaving and knew I wouldn't have to worry about them anymore. We drove away with those four girls waving at me. They looked jealous that I was leaving and that they had to remain behind.

CHAPTER SEVEN

❖❖❖   ❖❖❖   ❖❖❖   ❖❖❖

A New Life

MY LIFE CHANGED DRASTICALLY FOR the better when I went home with my father. In the years since my parents had divorced, he had stopped drinking as much as he had, although he still would have one or two drinks a night. I don't remember where or how he and Mom Barb met, but when they married in Point Comfort, Texas, where Mom Barb's family lived, we kids went to their wedding. I was seven when they married. This was the first time us kids had met Mom Barb. We had not seen our father for a few years. During the week we were there, my father, my new grandfather. and I went on a fishing and shrimp-catching trip. I caught a four-pound flounder, the biggest any of us caught. Though I was young and my first time fishing, my dad made me pull it in all by myself. That was the first trip I took to meet my new grandparents, and the last time I recall seeing my dad until he found me at the state school at the age of fifteen. After I had moved in with him and Mom Barb permanently, though, I saw my "new" grandparents several more times.

My dad treated me like his little princess, and my stepmother, Barb, was a great mother. She treated me with kindness and always had a hug and kiss for me. Sometimes I would help her with dinner, and we would talk about things that we wanted to do or what happened during the day at school or at home. She was funny, and I enjoyed the time I had with her. She would let me have anything I wanted, so I was very spoiled by her.

We lived in a beautiful home in Alvin, Texas, a small town just south of Houston. The house sat on a large corner lot, and the street made a complete circle with only one entrance. Our house had three bedrooms, a bath and a half, with a large living room and a kitchen/dining room next to it. Down the hall from the living room were the bedrooms, and I was able to decorate mine any way I wanted. (I was very proud of it too.) Outside by the kitchen door was the carport and driveway where Mom Barb's car, a Ford Thunderbird, and my father's 1960s-something Chevy pickup, three speed on the steering column, were parked. (My father would later try to teach me to drive in that old truck, but because it was a standard, I usually only make it about a foot from where I started. After several tries, Mom Barb then taught me how to drive her car, an automatic.)

My father loved the ballet, and we went to three performances in Houston. Mom Barb and I would go buy the prettiest dresses to wear, and then she would fix my hair to perfection. She also taught me how to apply makeup so it accented my face. I always felt pretty when we went. Dad would first take us to a nice restaurant and then to the performance, telling us it was a nightout for his girls. I began to enjoy the ballet as much as he did.

My father had a very good job as an electrician, and Mom Barb stayed home and managed the household. She would take me clothes shopping, often buying me only the best. I was in the ninth grade then, and it was the first time the other students at school didn't make fun of me. I ended up becoming very popular, making many friends, hanging out with the most liked girls, and dating only the popular boys. All our families, mine as well as my friends, had money. Life was wonderful! My parents treated me kindly, and I felt safe at home. I finally wasn't being bullied by my peers and was loved to the point of being spoiled rotten.

We had dinner every night together (Mom Barb was a great cook), and I would tell my parents all about my day at school or the new boy I had a crush on. My dad would talk about his day at work, whether good or bad, and Mom Barb would tell us what she had done, as well as ask us what we wanted for dinner the next few days. My favorite was her fried chicken. Yum! (Dad was more of a beef-and-potatoes guy.) Then we'd sit in the living room and watch TV or just talk. Dad encouraged me to get out with my friends and go to school dances. He didn't even mind me taking rides in my guy friends' trucks on weekends. I finally felt like I was part of a family that was *mine*.

Of course, even though dad treated me like a princess, I didn't always act like one. The only spanking I ever received was because I lied. Mom Barb had taken me shopping to buy me a beautiful new dress for a school dance. But instead of going to the dance, we teenagers went to the beach in Galveston, an hour away from Alvin. My dad found out through a friend he worked with. His daughter went to school with me, and she had gone to the dance. When she got home, she told her father that she didn't see me there. He told my father the first thing the next day. Dad spanked me, and Mom Barb hit him in the back because she thought he had spanked me too hard. Dad must have agreed because he later apologized. He didn't need to, though; I had deserved to be punished and was big enough a hard spanking was needed. I had lied, and I knew that was wrong, especially after they had treated me so well. Despite this punishment, though, I felt very loved and safe with them.

I had been living with my dad and Mom Barb for less than a year when I had a nervous breakdown. I'm not sure what triggered it, though I do remember feeling overwhelmed with sadness. When I first arrived, we had discussed a few times the rapes Willie had forced on me, but that was all. We didn't talk about how he had terrorized me. (When my father learned what Willie had done to me, he was furious and wanted to kill him.) I remember some of the details of my breakdown but didn't realize that it lasted for three days. All I remember is sitting on my bed rocking back and forth, and crying so hard I would throw up several times a day. If I wasn't crying, I was sleeping. Mom Barb came into my room and tried to comfort me, but I was inconsolable.

Concerned about my mental health, my father decided I needed professional help, so he took me to see Dr. Jill, a psychiatrist in Galveston. The hospital was about seventy miles from our house. In addition to our meeting with the doctor, the first appointment also allowed her to show us the unit within the hospital where she worked, and where I would be staying should my father decide to admit me, an option that should have happened later. However, after hearing the details of my breakdown, Dr. Jill suggested I be admitted that day to her pediatric lock unit in Jeannie Sealy. My father agreed, but neither of my parents had said anything about this possibility, probably because I would have thrown a fit about it. They were right. When they told me I would be staying, I was devastated by their decision and begged them to take me home with them. I cried for the first few days and wouldn't participate in any activities. Dr. Jill advised my parents not to visit me for a few months so I could adjust to the new environment. But when she felt I could handle it, they came to see me every weekend. Once I got used to being there, I worked on getting better by talking in my weekly one-on-one counseling sessions and nightly group meetings.

The Jeannie Sealy unit was located on the top (fifth) floor of the hospital, arranged as a long, wide hall. One end had four rooms for the boys, and the other end four rooms for the girls. In between was the communal dining/kitchen/TV area, as well as the staff office. At the first sight of this place, I felt sick. The color was very dull, and the air was filled with cigarette smoke. All the patients and some of the staff smoked.

Despite this initial reaction, the staff seemed wonderful and wanted me to feel better about being there. All were supportive and kind. Like anywhere else, though, I did have my favorites. One was a Jamaican woman who corn-rolled my hair. It would take her hours because my hair was so long, and, as she worked, I loved to hear her talk with her accent, telling me stories about her life in Jamaica. I could listen to her for a whole day and not get bored. I would leave the braids in for a few days, and my hair would be so curly! Then she would add tiny bows to the front of my head, flattening out a small portion of my hair on both sides, making me look beautiful. She loved playing with my hair and putting it up or just brushing it; it was comforting to me. To this day, I love having my hair played with. My second favorite staff member was a short elderly woman who had the brightest green eyes. She was always laughing, and it was a joy to be around her. I did like the rest of the staff, but those two were my favorites.

Most of the kids in Jeannie Sealy were my age, fifteen, or sixteen. And as with most groups, there were leaders, though this time, they weren't bullies. They acted just as kind and caring as the staff. This interaction between all of us *was* more family-oriented. On Saturday nights, we would all gather around to watch late-night TV. This was my favorite night of the week since all the patients were able to stay up late, eat popcorn, and drink as many sodas as we could take in. The rest of the week, except Friday, we had to be in bed early for school, located in the last four rooms of the girls' hallway.

School classes had a mixture of boys and girls. We would exercise for a half an hour in the mornings and then again in the evenings. We girls made up a song about our counterparts, the boys of Jeannie Sealy Five West, about how much we loved and appreciated them—and we did! Soon after, the guys made up their own song about how much they loved us. We trusted one another with our innermost thoughts and feelings without fearing judgment. It truly was a family atmosphere.

There were several different levels of privileges we had to earn. One of the first was being able to go outside with a staff member to the next building for our counseling sessions. (Otherwise, the meetings took place in a small room in the girls' part of the unit.) The next privilege allowed us to go outside with staff to have physical education, where we played baseball or volleyball. Following that, we could then go on outings to the beach or park with two staff members. The final freedom let us go to counseling meetings unescorted by anyone. The last two privileges were to prepare us to go home. We would then have several day outings with our parents over a three-month period, followed by weekend visits at our homes with our parents, again over a three-month period.

We had three square meals a day, and our classes went from 8:00 a.m. to 2:00 p.m. with quiet time until 3:00 p.m. We would study until dinner at 5:00 p.m. or until we finished our homework. I studied hard and became a straight A student. I focused on school and loved it. I was the only person in Algebra II, and both my parents and I were very proud of my accomplishments. As a result, my self-esteem began to rise and, with it, the idea that maybe I wasn't as dumb as everyone said (or thought) I was. I finally started feeling like I could make it through life.

After schoolwork was done, we could then watch TV or play cards or board games. The two large tables in the dining area, in an L shape, were used for all these activities, so we were never far from one another. Group meetings were at 6:00 p.m. and lasted sometimes until 8:00 p.m., then off to bed. Every day and every week had the same schedule.

The four rooms we had were large and comfortable and were primarily used for sleeping. Normally, there were two patients to a room. Each room was set up the same with two beds, two nightstands, two large windows where we could see the ocean and the other large buildings around us, and a bathroom. With permission from the staff, we could rearrange our furniture. We were allowed to have a few plants, and we could decorate our side of the room with posters and pictures. Staff were lenient about what we put up, although no nudity was allowed.

One of the most important rules of the unit was that we were not allowed to separate ourselves from the rest of the patients. We were *always* to interact with one another, and I think this is what made us so close. All of us would spend time with one another on a daily basis, so no cliques ever formed.

I stayed in this hospital for about a year and a half. I wasn't on any medication other than birth control, but with every group and individual counseling session, I began to learn tools to help me cope with the nightmare I had lived through. I can't really remember the first few months I was there because of the effects of my breakdown. But then Samantha, one of the other patients, confronted me about acting "sweet and innocent." I didn't have a clue as to what she was talking about, but she eventually helped me out of my shell. By this, I mean I was able to start seeing myself for what I truly was: a messed-up child. She would talk to me every day and ask me questions about what I liked to do or what some of my interests were, helping me find out who I was on the inside. I even found interests I didn't know I had. She did this in a loving, caring way, not mean or hateful like I had experienced at other places. As a result, I began to improve.

My parents could tell I was beginning to talk about the abuse from Joan and the rapes I had endured from Willie since I was starting to be more positive than negative. I could feel love again and was learning to trust others.

Despite this, however, I did run away once for more than two months. While at this hospital, I met and fell in love with the man who would be my first husband and the father of my oldest son. It was because of him that I ran away. When I was found, I was returned to the facility, only to be released a few months later. Despite all the improvements I had made, though, after I left, my life once again began to spiral out of control.

CHAPTER EIGHT

❖❖❖ ❖❖❖ ❖❖❖ ❖❖❖

Jose

I MET JOSE WHEN I had been at Jeannie Sealy about six months. His parents had brought him in one night in a very violent state. The staff had had to hold him down on the floor while they gave him Thorazine (a very strong drug that will render the person noncombative) in order to calm him down enough to safely handle him. He was immediately placed in isolation and remained there a week before he was allowed to be in with the rest of us.

The first time I saw Jose, I couldn't believe how handsome he was. About six feet tall with a muscular build, topped with shoulder-length dark-brown hair and brown eyes, he seemed perfect. I could tell he had some Latin in him because of his brown skin. We learned later he was sixteen years old. He told us he had been put in the unit because he had eaten too many "magic mushrooms" (these are mushrooms found under cow manure that make a person hallucinate). He had eaten so many that the hallucinations began freaking him out, making him uncontrollable and violent. He began seeing ants and other bugs all over his body that he kept trying to get off, so his parents had brought him in for evaluation. During his first few weeks, he kept arguing and fighting with the staff, so he ended up spending most of his time back in isolation. He later confessed to me he did it because he liked the drugs they would then give him.

When Jose was finally placed in a room and allowed to be in with the rest of us, we would talk and spend time together at the dining-room tables, playing cards and board games. On Saturday nights, we always sat by each other and held hands while watching late-night TV. He seemed to be as attracted to me as I was him. I was shy at the time, so he sought me out. My dad and Mom Barb hated him; they would tell me every time they came to see me that he was no good for me and asked the staff to keep us separated. They did, but it solved nothing.

For most of the time we were on the unit together, we were not allowed to talk to each other or sit next to each other. The staff members, as well as Dr. Jill, said we spent too much time together, isolating ourselves from the others. They called our relationship "toxic," with Jose being the "bad boy" and me being the "good girl." They said we needed to associate more with our peers, in order to keep the family atmosphere. But since we enjoyed each other's company more than that of any of the others, we would seek each other out instead of finding someone else. Plus, as teenagers, having adults tell us we couldn't see each other only made us want to see each other more, and it was primarily the adults' dislike of our relationship that made our attraction for each other unstoppable.

The last straw for Jose came when he sneaked into my room through the hallway between the boys' and girls' halls to spend time with me. I didn't know he was coming. After we took a shower together and had sex, he told me he had figured out how to open the windows from the inside and that we could use sheets tied together to climb down and escape. He wanted me to run away with him so we could be together without any adult interference. Though we were on the fifth floor and the ledge under the windows was only about six inches wide, he showed me how we could get out by climbing out onto that ledge. After climbing back in, he kept the staff out by using my and my roommate's beds to barricade the door. He then spent the time trying to talk me into leaving with him, but I couldn't go along.

I was just too afraid to get out on that ledge. There was nothing but concrete under it, and if I slipped, I was sure the fall would be fatal.

Meanwhile, my roommate, who was on a lot of drugs, stood in the corner of our room crying and screaming for the staff. Jose had threatened to beat her up if she moved the beds. After the staff had been beating on the door and yelling for us to let them in for over an hour, I finally did by moving one of the beds out of the way (it was during all this commotion that Jose had tried to talk me into escaping with him). One of my favorite staff members, the short older lady with the beautiful green eyes, came in first. The disappointment on her face crushed me. She didn't say a word to me. I wish she would have; it would have hurt less than the look. A male staff member grabbed Jose and took him straight too solitary; I could hear him laughing all the way. About a week later, he was sent home. He had been on the unit for about six months, and I didn't ever think I would see him again. I was placed on room restriction, and I didn't see him before he left, but we were able to exchange notes with the help of other kids. I cried often, and the thought of never seeing him again devastated me.

But then he began writing, and when the first letter came, I cried. I was so happy he'd been thinking about me and missed me as much as I missed him. He wrote me every day, wanting me to come to see him. He called at least once a week to hear my voice. My parents tried to have the communication stopped, but staff continued to allow it. Consequently, within three months of Jose leaving, I ran away in an attempt to be with him.

The perfect opportunity presented itself in a day trip to Galveston beach with my dad and Mom Barb. The decision was spontaneous since I was still angry with them for keeping Jose and me apart. I walked down the beach a few hundred yards and began talking to several young people who were drinking; they had traveled from Dallas in order to spend the day at the beach. Most were in their early twenties. I started drinking with them and decided to go back with them to Mesquite, Texas, on the outskirts of Dallas. I told them I was a runaway and wanted to go to Kemah to see my boyfriend. Going to Mesquite meant going way out of my way and farther north than I wanted to go, but since they said they would let me stay with them until they could afford to drive me to Kemah where Jose lived, I decided to go for it. One of the guys promised me he would make sure I would get there even though that meant driving about two hundred miles. But because they all worked, I had to wait two weeks before they could make the trip, despite my begging them daily to take me sooner. Those two weeks seemed like an eternity.

But they finally took me, dropping me off at Jose's parents' house. Though Kemah is a relatively small town on Galveston Bay, where most people worked on the sea either taking people out deep-sea fishing or working on fishing or shrimping boats, I still had a hard time finding Jose. But then I saw him in the middle of the street in front of his friend's house. When he saw me, he started running to me with a big smile on his face while I froze at the sight of him. The first question he asked me was why I hadn't written him for the last few weeks? I answered his question by telling him of my running away and having to wait before I could come to him. We were in Kemah for about four weeks. We couldn't live with his parents because his mother didn't like me and refused to let me stay in her home. He was the baby of the family, and no one was good enough for her son. So for most of the time, we stayed at various friends' houses until we wore out our welcome. Finally, we decided to go to Marion and stay at Joan's house. We called her and told her of our situation, and she agreed to let us stay with her. Since I was still on the run from the psychiatric unit, Jose reasoned it would be the last place anyone would look for me.

Our stay at Joan's was just what I thought it would be: miserable. She was as hateful to me as she had been in the past. Izzy was five or six, and she and I got along. I considered my little sister at this time. We stayed a total of four weeks, and with Willie in prison during this time, Joan complained about food and money every day. Jose did do odd jobs around town, but Joan constantly told him he needed to find a job so he could take care of me. She finally talked him into joining the Marines, saying that would provide stability for us. Before he signed up, though, we decided to go back to Kemah to gather his belongings and inform his family of his decision. All of us—Jose, me, Joan, and Izzy—made the trip.

Somehow (I suspect Jose's mother called them) my dad and Mom Barb learned we were there, and Dad called their house wanting to speak to me. When I took the call, he tried to talk me into going back to the hospital, but I refused. With Jose going into the Marines, we were planning on our future together, and being apart from him wasn't a choice I wanted to make at the time. However, shortly after I hung up, the police pulled into their driveway with my parents behind them. They arrested me and released me to my parents' custody without going to the police station. Then they told me they were taking me back to Galveston, saying it was for my own good. I was furious with them and got into a screaming match with them with Jose, standing next to me, joining in. It didn't do any good, though. They took me anyway.

When I returned to the psychiatric hospital, Dr. Jill placed me on restriction, meaning all my privileges were taken from me, and I was not allowed to leave the unit. Within a few weeks, though, they let me have most of my privileges back without my having to ask for them. I could walk to my counseling sessions alone, go outside on group trips, and go on outings with my parents again. They knew I couldn't get to Jose easily; he was too far away, about 150 miles. Even though I no longer wanted to be at the facility, neither did I try to run away. Nothing mattered to me other than Jose and being with him.

I spent my sixteenth birthday there. Joan and Izzy came to see me that day, but Jose couldn't because he wasn't allowed on the unit. I was about half a year from my seventeenth birthday when they released me a few months after my return, so they let me decide with whom I wanted to live. I opted for Joan since I was very angry at my dad and Mom Barb for separating Jose and me, and I didn't want to go back to live with them. I had also learned that Jose was living with Joan, and I still wanted to be with him.

Looking back now, I can remember some warning signs I should have seen. I knew Jose was letting another girl on the unit play with his penis when we were not allowed to talk or sit next to each other.

Plus, he always seemed to be interested in other girls more than me. Whenever he became angry, he would turn vicious, becoming violent and using abusive language toward those who angered him. However, he didn't start expressing it toward me until we lived at Joan's house the first time before I returned to the hospital. Still, I traded the positive growth, care, and affirmation I had been receiving from my parents and the staff at Jeannie Sealy for a verbally abusive mother and boyfriend. I was used to the verbal abuse and thought this was a "normal" part of a relationship. Despite all the positive support I had received, I didn't feel like I deserved anything better than what Joan and Jose gave me. Everything I had worked so hard for—my grades, myself esteem, and the work I had put into getting better—went out the window just to have someone, anyone, love me. But because I didn't realize that what Jose gave me wasn't true love, I didn't put myself first—or anywhere for that matter. Jose was everything to me. Whatever he wanted, he got, just as long as he stayed with me, even if that meant sharing him sexually with my "friends." The physical abuse only started when I would tell him no to something he wanted. He was used to getting his way.

After my return to Jeannie Sealy, Jose decided to continue living with Joan and Izzy in Marion. After my release, we stayed in Joan's trailer for three of four months. She again talked him into joining the Marines, so he and I once again made the trip back to Kemah. Only this time, it was to party with his friends before he left for boot camp. Since he hadn't actually officially joined the Marines yet, we ended up spending more time there than I had expected. Within a few months, I became pregnant with my first child. For the first three months, though, I didn't realize it, so I kept using drugs, primarily speed. But I stopped as soon as I learned that I was pregnant. I hadn't had a monthly cycle in three months, so Jose decided to buy me a pregnancy test from the local drugstore. We had been living with his family about two weeks, and I was four months pregnant before Jose finally joined the Marines and went to boot camp. He had to take me back to Joan because his family didn't want to take care of me.

It was while living at Kemah that Jose began the abusive behavior that lasted the rest of our relationship. While I was pregnant, he'd leave me alone in the apartment we stayed in before we moved in with his parents, as he went out drinking with other women. The woman manager of our building would come to our apartment wanting Jose to come to her house so she could "talk to him." I don't know what happened, but if I had to guess, they were having sex with each other. She'd do this even if I answered the door. Then if I argued with him or disagreed with anything he said, he would throw beer on me. If he thought a woman was pretty, he'd let her know. Even if I was with him, he'd give her all his attention, totally ignoring me. And it didn't matter if she was married or had a boyfriend. This hurt me deeply, but whenever I would tell him that it did, he'd become very angry and start verbally abusing me. His favorite thing to tell me was, I was just jealous and so what if other women were attracted to him? It was my problem, and I needed to fix myself, not him. Looking back, I don't recall him ever telling me I was beautiful, only pretty, and I don't remember him saying he loved me.

The three months I spent with Joan while Jose attended boot camp in San Diego, California, were long ones. Almost immediately after we had taken Jose to the airport, she started acting like she hated me. Her voice always had hatred in it when she would speak to me, and she acted like it was a chore just to say one sentence to me. She had gotten me a job at the furniture factory where she worked, but because I was pregnant, I was unable to do the task they gave me. I used a staple gun to fasten cloth to the frame of furniture that was attached to an air hose that had a lot of power and was hard for me to control. Also, it was hot in the factory. There was no air-conditioning, and the work was hard. After a few days, I quit, and Joan became angry with me. She said she didn't have enough income to keep all three of us, so I needed to help with the expenses. Jose sent some money, but not very often and not enough. So I applied for welfare and food stamps to help out, but that still wasn't good enough in Joan's eyes. The doctor I saw was at the free clinic, so my vitamins and visits were free. The only bills Joan had were for an air-conditioner she had purchased because she didn't have one, electric, gas for her car, and food. I don't know how much money she made, but her bills couldn't have added up to more than three hundred dollars a month.

During my seventh month of pregnancy, Jose came home after finishing boot camp and stayed for four weeks. We took a trip for two weeks to see his friends and family in Kemah until we had to return so I could see my doctor. While staying with Joan, Jose and I would walk two miles every day to help my delivery be easier. I loved doing macramé, and he would help me to get a new hanger started by putting the jute through the ring so I wouldn't have to stretch my arms up. At the end of the four weeks, Jose returned to California and his new station at Oceanside. I couldn't go with him because I was too far along in my pregnancy to fly. Later, after giving birth and moving to Oceanside with him, he told me what I think is the reason Joan hated me so much. When Jose had stayed with her while I was returned to Jeannie Sealy, he said she had been having sex with him but couldn't after my release. I believed him because he seemed ashamed of it. I asked her about it, but she denied it—and still does. I was devastated.

I gave birth to my first on August 4, 1980, in San Antonio. Jose had wanted him named after him, so he became Jose Jr. (calling him JJ). I stayed with Joan for two more weeks before flying to California. When I was getting off the plane, Jose's first words to me were, "You're fat and need to lose weight." Then he said he wanted to hold JJ.

The apartment he had rented (and that we had to share with a roommate) had two bedrooms, one bath, a large living room, and a small patio. The kitchen was large for an apartment with lots of cabinets. Our roommate was a tall, skinny redhead who wore glasses. He was kind to me and loved JJ and would often take me and JJ on rides to Hollywood and the beach when Jose would go out into the field two weeks at a time. JJ was a sweet child, full of smiles, and I thought everything would be better for me now and that having a child together would bring Jose and me closer together. It actually made our relationship worse. Shortly after moving to California with him, Jose started sleeping with other women he had met before I got to Oceanside. He also wanted to be able "threesomes" sex with me and, at the same time, with those friends I had met in the apartment complex. He also renewed his flirting with other women and acting the way he had while in Texas.

Despite this, we finally married on October 9, 1980. I had agreed to it because Jose had explained to me that if we married, he could make more money. Then we could move into another apartment by ourselves, away from all the chaos and parties. Since the roommate was single, he would have friends over on the weekends, and just about every Saturday, there would be three or four guys passed out in our living room. I wanted more privacy for myself and JJ, even though Jose didn't seem to mind the chaos.

Once again, I believed this change—moving into our own apartment—would improve our relationship. But, once again, it didn't. Jose's abuse became even worse, and he began to be violent, hitting me daily, though never in the face. He said I was too pretty to hit in the face, but the rest of my body was fair game and was soon covered with bruises. I don't remember any of the reasons he gave me for hitting me, but it made me feel like I was a bad person who was somehow responsible for his behavior. He'd repeatedly tell me that it was my fault he hit me and that I was the one making him angry enough to do it. He beat me so much that some days I was so sore it was hard for me to move around. This violent behavior became worse, and his punches became harder.

Occasionally, some of Jose's buddies from the base would come over to our apartment and spend the weekend with us, giving them a chance to get away from the barracks and have some fun partying. One weekend, Tim, one of these friends, saw Jose pulling me through the apartment by my hair, caveman-style, dragging me into the bedroom. He grabbed Jose by his shirt and pulled him out on the large patio, where he began hitting him with his fist. Tim told him he had no business hitting me, and if he was angry, he should pick on someone his own size.

This wasn't the only time Tim witnessed Jose's abuse. He also noticed the bruises from previous beatings. Whenever Tim was around, Jose left me alone because he knew Tim would protect me. Consequently, I always wanted him around, and we became good friends. He would talk to me and try to convince me to leave Jose, saying he didn't want me to be hurt anymore. I believed that *I* was the problem. I thought if I could only do better, he would stop hitting me. He and Jose often fought each other out on the patio because of me, and sometimes the fights would last for several minutes because neither one would give in. When this happened, their other friends would have to break them up.

Despite (or possible because of) Tim's warnings and physical attacks, Jose continued to abuse me. He once became so angry with me—I can't remember why—that he put all five hundred pounds of the weights on his weightlifting bar and tied me to it by my wrists with rope. At only 120 pounds, I couldn't move it at all. He left me there for almost two days, raping and hitting me. He even threatened me by pointing his shotgun in my face and telling me it was for my own good and that JJ deserved a better mother than me. All I could think about was JJ. Jose said he could take care of him without me, and I became paralyzed with fear that my baby wouldn't have a mother.

Now terrified of this man, I finally decided to leave him. Joan had recently moved to Ridgecrest, California, about 250 miles from Oceanside, to be closer to her father, so I moved back in with her. When I told her of the abuse I was going through, she agreed to let me stay with her. She wasn't happy about my decision to leave Jose and tried more than once to talk me into going back to him. Being Catholic, she would tell me it is a sin to get a divorce, even though I was being beaten. And with Willie in prison, I felt safer staying with her.

For the next year, I did go back to Jose about five times, but I would always have to leave again because of his abuse and move back in with Joan. Though he loved JJ and always treated him well, I would take him with me whenever I left. These back-and-forth trips finally ended when I returned to high school and started working part-time at Burger King while living with Joan. I was eighteen at the time and had enrolled in Mesquite High, a continuation school for teen mothers who wanted to continue their education while pregnant or after giving birth. The other students, girls who were not mothers and the boys, had been placed there for various reasons. It proved to be a great experience, as well as a favorable mix, for me, and I made several lifelong friends. I took classes that helped me prepare for my GED. When I took the test, I passed it with no problems.

I became especially close to three of my classmates while at Mesquite High, although I had several good friends. Lori, Debbie, Mel, and I had a lot in common. They became my best friends; I still keep in contact with them and enjoy having them in my life. Lori especially loved JJ and, since she spent a great deal of time with us, became like a second mother to him. Debbie, Mel, and I, on the other hand, spent a lot of time at parties. The close friendship of all three helped me through some of the hard times I had while living in Ridgecrest and Joan. They could see the hate-filled resentment she had toward me and so would not hesitate to stand by me any situation. All of them could tell she despised me. When I would go back and forth to Jose, they consoled me about the abuse I'd just been through. When I had my heart broken by a boy, they all comforted me, especially Lori. I spent some of the best times of my life with them.

When I learned that Willie would soon be released from prison, I decided to go to back to Jose. Though I hadn't seen Willie in over three years, I was still very much afraid of him and didn't want to be anywhere near him. Therefore, I chose the lesser of two evils. However, because Jose had been dishonorably discharged from the Marines for selling drugs on the base, we had to return to Texas to live with his parents. Though I didn't really want to move back to Kemah, I was glad to be putting many hundreds of miles between me and Willie.

Jose and I lived with his parents. His dad was wonderful, his mother not so much. Jose's dad would talk to me with kindness in his voice and even taught me how to make perfect pancakes. His mother, on the other hand, would always treat me with hatefulness, like Joan did, and would make me feel unwanted in her home. But she never treated Jose that way. After we'd been there a few months, I finally got fed up.

Jose had gotten a job working on a fishing boat, and his boss had invited us for dinner and drinks at his house so he could meet

JJ and me. But on the way home, with JJ in the back seat asleep, I started arguing with Jose about his flirting with his boss's daughter, who was sixteen, and he became angry. Suddenly he drove to the side of the road, reached over me to open the passenger-side door, and pushed me out of the moving car. Since I wasn't expecting it and wasn't wearing a seat belt and because he was so strong, I went tumbling out of the car into a ditch he had gotten close to. Stunned that he had done this and in pain from the fall, I started crying. I limped to an IHOP restaurant, the closest business that was open, about a block away. I used their pay phone to call Jose's father, who came and picked me up. On the way back, he refused to talk about what happened, saying he didn't want to get involved with our problems. Feeling hopeless and afraid, I cried the whole way back to Kemah, twelve miles away.

Jose was at the house by the time we got there. When his mother learned what had happened, she came into our room and told me I deserved what I got. Jose was also in the room, and when he heard what she said, he laughed. I was so sore from the fall out of the car I couldn't get out of bed for a few days. Even though his mother knew that, she still accused me of being neglectful because I wasn't caring for my child.

That was the last straw. I had finally had enough of being bullied, beaten, and berated, especially when I had done nothing to deserve it. My dad convinced me to leave and move into the dorms where he staying, but I knew if I did, I'd have to leave JJ because children weren't allowed. (After returning to Texas, I reached out to my father by phone after being treated horrible by Jose when we first got back. I had been talking to him for two months when the car incident happened. He and Mom Barb had gotten a divorce, though I don't why we never discuss it, and he had sold his house. He had begun taking classes at the University of Houston and had taken a job caring for a paralyzed man, who was also a student at the school. He was doing well in his classes and enjoyed going to school.) I didn't want to leave JJ, but I had no other choice. Jose's beatings were getting worse and more frequent, and he had threatened that if I ever took his son away from him, he'd kill me. He didn't really care about me; he just thought as long as he could threaten me that way, I'd stay with him. But I just couldn't. I couldn't take the beatings anymore.

So though it hurt me to the core, with my heart breaking, I took JJ to the sitter's and told him I'd be back even though I knew I wouldn't. Once I had a job and a place to live, I had hoped to return to Kemah to get him. But before I could, Joan had gone there and taken him from Jose because he could no longer care for him. He called her and told her to come get him. For two years, I would call her and cry, telling Joan how much I missed my son. All the time, she had him with her and never told me. Since Joan took JJ, Jose had never paid a dime of child support and was never again been part of my son's life.

Lest you think my relationship with Jose was all bad, we did have a few good times, especially when we rode his Triumph chopper. He loved that machine more than life and was very proud of it. We would take trips into the California Mountains with friends and camp out. Riding that motorcycle and being outside in the fresh air did us both good, and Jose would treat me like I mattered to him. Before we'd leave, he'd braid my long hair so it wouldn't get tangled. He'd always say, "You have to have a pretty girl on the back of your bike that knows how to ride!" That always made me feel good, like I really was pretty. Sometimes, as we rode along, he would encourage me to "flash" the truckers going by. I did once, and he giggled like a small child. He liked for other men to look at me; I think it made him feel proud that I was his.

During one of our trips to the mountains, we hit some loose gravel, and the back tire slid out from under us, laying the bike down. Jose hurt his knee from the weight of me and the bike, and I had terrible road rash on my right leg and hip. Despite his own pain, he made sure I had medical attention as soon as he could. I walked on crutches for a week, and he catered to my every need. I know he felt guilty, a feeling he only had twice in our marriage.

Finally, on March 6, 1987, Jose and I were officially divorced. I had filed while living in Ridgecrest, California. After seeing it three years later, he refused to believe it. His reason: he had not received divorce papers.

CHAPTER NINE

❖❖❖   ❖❖❖   ❖❖❖   ❖❖❖

Acting Out

AFTER LEAVING JOSE BUT BEFORE we were legally divorced, I moved into the dorms at the university where my dad attended. I was nineteen. While I lived there, I started topless dancing and worked in the bars for three and half years. This turned out to be a good as well as a bad time in my life. The first time I got on stage though, I had to drink many beers and a few whiskey shots to be numb enough so I wouldn't be sick to my stomach from the way the men looked at me. I hated all of them.

Each time I danced, my conscience would become increasingly deadened not just from the alcohol but from me not caring about myself anymore. I felt like a throwaway, and that the only men who would ever want me were those older ones who just wanted a younger cute girlfriend to play around with. My new lifestyle included daily drug use, mainly cocaine, and trying new sexual acts, including homosexuality. (I quickly realized that wasn't for me.) I was also continually hurt from having to leave my child. Staying high and drunk kept the pain away for a while, but it would always eventually return.

My dad's major at college was psychology, and he had decided to write his thesis paper for his bachelor's degree on topless and nude dancers and their backgrounds. He was the one who talked me into dancing topless, thinking it would be a good way for me to make quick money as well as help me overcome my struggles with men. He also told me my dancing would be a good way to get back at men, though he never mentioned what it would do to me.

While researching his paper, my dad had met one of the DJs who played the music for the performers. He introduced me to him so he could teach me the ways of the business. One of the first rules I learned was never use you real name, so the DJ named me Havana because my dark skin made me look Hispanic or Latin. I picked up all the other rules quickly, like hustling for money by giving table dances to both male and female customers, finding regular customers who would only ask for me to sit at their table, and having men buy me drinks. (They contained very little alcohol, and we dancers made a commission off any drinks sold this way.)

Most of the money, though, wasn't made on stage but in what we called boom-booming. After performing, we'd go down into the crowd, still topless, and dance in front of the men at the bar. Some would try to touch me, but I would quickly slap their hands away. Most customers wouldn't tip while we were on stage, but they did if we got up close to them. I made 90 percent of my money doing this, earning around two hundred dollars a night. Back in the '80s, this was not a bad day's pay.

To keep us "fresh", the different clubs rotated the performers between them, so I'd usually work only three or four days a week. While most of the other dancers used their money to buy nice cars or houses or to put themselves through college, I used mine to buy cocaine, eventually becoming addicted to it. I was tired of hurting all the time, and it seemed that nothing else would take the pain away. And even that didn't help; when the drugs wore off, all my heart (and soul) aches would return. My father told me that almost all of the dancers he had met had been either molested or raped when they were younger. In most cases, the abuse also affected their sexuality. I discovered he was right; most of the girls I danced with were lesbians, primarily because they didn't trust men.

The year after I began dancing, the National Football League went on strike, with all teams refusing to play. So the United States

Football League was formed with the Texas team being put together in Houston. Since I had always wanted to be a professional dancer *with* clothes, I decided to try out for their cheerleading squad. This was an amazing day!

At least four or five thousand other young women had the same thought and had gathered in the large ballroom in a local hotel where the tryouts were being held. After the choreographers showed us the dance we would be performing, they began calling us in groups of twenty. Each group would perform the dance that only took about a minute to execute. I ended up being one of the last to try out. After about four hours, I finally had my chance. Though I had no formal training, I loved to dance, but my body just wouldn't move the way they wanted it to. My coordination wasn't good enough, and I ended up losing my balance and falling. I was devastated! Not surprisingly, when they called the names of those who had been picked for the squad, mine was not one of them. I had wanted this so much, I cried.

While I worked as a dancer, I met some of the players of the NFL team in Houston, the members of a very popular rhythm and blues band, and some very wealthy men who had made their money from oil. The football players came into one of the fancier clubs I danced in. I ended up going on a few dates with one of them. He turned out to be a very nice guy! A few of the others I associated with though, one turned out not to be so nice when he became physically violent with me. (I never went out with him again.)

My roommate, a very beautiful woman, had entered the *Playboy* strip-off contest and was chosen to go to California for the taping of the finals. The R & B band had performed at that contest, and the lead singer became very attracted to her. When she returned to Houston, he contacted her and invited her to one of their concerts at the A&M College in College Station. She accepted and asked if I could come with her. He said I could, even paying for my plane ticket. We had front row seats and had a great time! We were invited to another concert in Dallas at the largest bar in Texas. This time though, because the place was packed, we stayed in the back while they performed. The last time we were together with the members of this band, we went to the Houston Rodeo at the astrodome. All of this was very exciting for me.

Toward the later part of my dancing career, I became involved with a cult called the Way. Three of their members had come into one of the clubs where I was working and witnessed to me. I thought that was a strange place for three young men to be seeking converts, but they showed love and compassion toward me, so I listened to what they had to say. It sounded pretty convincing, especially since I was in my early twenties, and very impressionable (and also because of all the abuse I had experienced), so I eventually moved in with several other members in a large three-story house. I was accepted very quickly into this group; that felt good to me since that had never happened before. They taught me how to speak in tongues and "rightly divide the word of God" by studying it. Though I had been baptized for eight years, my time with this cult actually began my active pursuit of the Lord. However, instead of studying on my own (what I learned to do later in life), I simply believed everything they told me. As a result, I made even more crucial mistakes in my life.

There seemed to be no morality in this cult since they considered my lifestyle to be all right. As a result of my promiscuity, though, I became pregnant by the DJ (Paul) at one of the clubs where I danced. (He was very handsome and treated me well.) I didn't tell him about the pregnancy, but I did tell the cult group. They talked me into having an abortion, and I've regretted it ever since having nightmares of a young adorable male child calling me Mommy.

When I told Paul about my abortion, he became very angry and said I should have talked with him first to see what he wanted to do since the child was his also. But because I didn't know what the Bible said, the cult members had convinced me that a baby isn't really alive until he takes his first breath. Of course, today I know that the Lord "knows us from our mother's womb." I believe my child is with the Lord and that someday I'll be able to tell him how very sorry I am for taking his life. After having the nightmares about my aborted child, I realized the decision I'd made wasn't what the Lord had wanted. I left the cult, knowing what they believed in wasn't correct. I moved in with friends and wasn't bothered by them anymore.

CHAPTER TEN

◇◇◇　　◇◇◇　　◇◇◇　　◇◇◇

James

AFTER LEAVING THE CULT, I went back to dancing, and it was during this time that I met James, my daughter Abigale's father. I was twenty-one at the time. Sue, my friend from Ridgecrest, had recently moved to Houston, and her boyfriend worked with James at a landscaping company. After having no contact with each other for about two years, we began talking on the phone. Eventually saying she wanted to visit me and I greatly looked forward to that day, we had dinner together, and I met her current boyfriend (whose name I have forgotten), the one who worked with James. A few days later, Sue called and asked if I wanted to meet a really nice guy who happened to be her boyfriend's coworker. I agreed, liked what I saw, and James and I soon began dating. Our relationship flourished after I got over being jealous of his previous girlfriend—a woman who was, to me, the prettiest one in Ridgecrest.

It turned out that Sue was right: James was a nice guy and very good to me, so I moved in with him. However, when I realized I had become pregnant, he wanted me to have an abortion. But because I was still emotionally hurting from my previous abortion, I couldn't do it, and he accepted my decision. He had known from the beginning that I had another child, and he asked questions about him, his age, where he lived, and why. He also knew Willie had raped me, but that was all. When I wanted JJ back, he paid for his plane ticket from California. He was five at the time, and Joan was not happy I wanted him with me. When I called her to let her know James had bought his ticket, she became angry but couldn't do anything about it because he wasn't her child. By the end of the conversation though, she did say she thought it would be good for JJ. Because I was pregnant, she thought it would help me to settle down.

James and I had only been together for about two months when I became pregnant, but we had become close. James had moved us into a nice area of Houston in a very nice two-bedroom, one-bath apartment, enough space for all four of us. (We had been living in a one-bedroom, one-bath apartment.) JJ had his own room, decorated just for him, and things he liked. Thankfully, he and James fell in love with each other, and James treated him as his own son. When James came home from work, he and JJ would play and wrestle in the living room while I made dinner. At bedtime, he'd read to him. Whenever we went grocery shopping, he would keep both of us entertained by juggling fruit, something JJ thought was uproariously funny. James took very good care of both of us.

While I was in this relationship, I had the immense privilege of befriending with James's mother, Nina. She became the mother I'd never had, as well as one of the most important people God put in my life. Everyone in my family called her Grandma from day one. She was (and still is) a committed, Spirit-filled Christian and Pentecostal preacher who, over time, guided me into more and more biblical truths. She specialized in spiritual warfare, believing there are good spirts as well as bad spirits, and that we as Christians have the power over bad spirits and their leader, the devil. Jesus gave us this power when he died on the cross for all of us. In her walk with God, Grandma became very knowledgeable in this area of the Bible. Time and time again, she has stood up to these bad spirts and has won, casting them out of people or making them leave someone's home. I have seen it myself. I found it amazing and impressive, and she shared her knowledge with me. We became—and still are—very close. We are so committed to each other that she calls me "Ruthie," and I call her "Naomi," from the story in the book of Ruth in the Bible. (And if you're unfamiliar with the story, read it. It's in the Old Testament and isn't very long.)

Shortly after I learned I was pregnant, I began attending a local church. The unconditional love I received from Grandma made me interested in learning more about Jesus. Letting go of the past mistakes I'd made was the beginning of my journey in this new life. The parishioners at the church also showed me unconditional love and helped me understand that God loved me in the same way. This is when I started studying the Bible on my own and learning the truths that were in it. The more I learned, the more I fell in love with the Lord. Consequently, my life changed for the better. I quit smoking, drinking, and taking drugs. I had more respect for myself and stopped dancing. To earn extra money, I started a carpool, taking the neighborhood kids back and forth to school.

I gave birth to Abigale on September 11, 1985 in Houston, Texas. (I was still married to Jose at the time.) She was six weeks premature, weighing only four and a half pounds, and because James's and my blood types were incompatible, she also had jaundice. Consequently, she had to stay in the hospital for the first two weeks of her life. (I'm thankful I hadn't been smoking, drinking, or taking drugs while pregnant with her.) My beautiful baby girl looked so small and helpless that I endured a three-hour bus ride every day so I could be by her side. James didn't think I had to be there *every* day, saying there were two other people who needed me. But since the doctors had given Abigale only a fifty-fifty chance of survival, I didn't want to miss a day of her life. James and JJ would go with me on the weekends. They both loved and adored her. She was so tiny, I could lay her head in the palm of my hand, and her feet would barely reach my elbow.

In the nursery intensive care unit, she was surrounded by machines that, even though I knew they were helping her live, still scared me. Because of her jaundice, she had to be under a bright light, with covers for her eyes that looked like sunglasses. We called her my "Hollywood baby." Lying under the light with the "sunglasses," she looked just like someone tanning herself. Those eye covers are still in her baby book, along with a very small bracelet she had on her tiny wrist. I love reliving her story and have told it to Abigale several times.

Nina remained a large part of my life even after James and I broke up. When Abigale (who ended up being her only grandchild) was born, I decided Grandma would always be in her life, and that if I kept her from her grandmother, I would be making a terrible mistake. She eventually became an important part of my whole family's life, praying for us every day and treating all us as her own.

Her husband, Melvin, also became very involved in our lives. We called him Grandpa, and he accepted all my children as his grandchildren, making sure he spent time with each of them. Of course, he thought Abigale was the best granddaughter in the world and could do no wrong. He has been the only grandfather she and JJ have ever known. My third husband, Peter, called him Pap, and several times they took JJ hunting and fishing with them.

For some reason, I decided I no longer wanted to be in this relationship with James. My heart just wasn't in it, though I'm not sure why. Maybe I had some hard feelings toward him because he wanted me to abort my daughter or maybe I just couldn't handle being treated well, or maybe because I had been abused so much, it was the subconscious stress of constantly wondering when the violence would begin. James knew about my marriage to Jose and the abuse I'd endured but didn't know all the details. Though we had been together just over a year, and though I was still married to Jose, the question of James and I getting married never came up. At any rate, I packed up my two children and took a bus back to Ridgecrest, California. We left the same day the shuttle blew up, and people talked about it the whole way. I left while James, who had no idea we were leaving, was at work, and I had taken the rent money to pay for the trip. I didn't talk to him for about a month, but when I contacted him, he wanted us to return to Houston. Later, I actually felt relieved that I hadn't married him since he turned out not to be the man I thought he was. He paid no child support until Abigale was sixteen years old and had nothing to do with his daughter's life.

Though he lived in the same town as she and his mother do, he still didn't visit her.

James has recently passed away. Despite my feelings about him, he ended up giving me two of the greatest gifts in my life, Grandma and Abigale. Thank you, James, and rest in peace.

CHAPTER ELEVEN

◇◇◇　　◇◇◇　　◇◇◇　　◇◇◇

Richard "Dick"

AFTER RETURNING TO RIDGECREST, AND once again living with Joan, I met my second husband, Dick. Because I was still married to Jose, I still had my military ID, so I used it to take the children to the base swimming pool in the summer. We had been in Ridgecrest about four months when I met Dick at the pool one day and started a conversation with him. He was in the Navy stationed at China Lake Naval Weapons Center right next to Ridgecrest. I don't recall the conversation, but he didn't seem to mind that I had two young children, so we started going out on dates. I didn't commit to him right away though; I dated two other sailors while I was dating him. However, one only wanted to have sex with me, and the other, though very handsome, had many other girlfriends. Since I was looking some who only wanted one girlfriend at a time, I decided to give a relationship with Dick a try.

So all of us—JJ, Abigale, Dick, and I—moved off base into a trailer in town. He had nice furniture and a huge stereo, and I was impressed by his stories of traveling to exotic places, like Hong Kong. His face would light up whenever he'd speak of his adventures spending hours telling me where each of his several souvenirs of his travels had come from. I was so amazed by all the places he'd been overseas and enjoyed listening to him.

Despite my break from alcohol, I picked it up again from being with Dick. There was a bar near our house, and we would leave JJ and Abigale in the care of the older brother of one of JJ's friends. (JJ was six at the time, and the brother was twelve) These two boys were the only kids in the neighborhood and came over often to play, so I knew them well enough to watch him and Abigale. But then we began drinking every daily, and Dick started to have controlling behavior. But because I didn't want to move back with Joan, especially since I knew Willie would soon be released from prison, I decided to ignore these warning signs.

After about a year of living with Dick, he was transferred to the naval base in San Diego and asked if I would go with him. I said I would, since my only other alternative was to return to Joan. However, my feelings for the man were gone, and I only agreed to go with him to get out of Ridgecrest. But I also thought it would be a great opportunity for the children and me, giving me a chance to go to college, something I had always wanted to do so I could better myself for my family. (I could have started my basic credit hours at the community college in Ridgecrest, but I didn't know that at the time.) The best part of the move though was being able to go to the beach, one of my favorite places. I loved going there, and the thought of being able to take my children so they could experience it too made me very happy.

After moving to San Diego, about two months later, Dick asked me to marry him. I said no, giving for my reason the fact that I didn't love him and that I felt he was too much of a controller. But he didn't seem to care about my feelings, only that if I married him, he'd receive more money from the military. Then he told me if I didn't marry him, he'd send me back to Ridgecrest to live with Joan again, even though he knew Willie had just been released from prison. He had known Joan and my situation from the beginning, had seen the fights between us and, and a few months later, had learned I'd been raped by Willie. I couldn't believe he'd threaten me with sending me back in that situation. He insisted he needed the pay increase to take care of all of us on what he currently received, though I thought we were financially okay. I called Joan and spent hours trying to explain the reasons I didn't want to marry Dick—that I didn't love him, that he dominated me, that everything in me felt I would be making a mistake if I did—but none of that mattered to her. She felt it would be good security for me and my children. Plus, she really didn't want me back in her house with Willie there. According to her, he'd been out of prison less than two months and had already committed another rape. I once again thought I had no choice but to pick between the lesser of two evils.

So on March 18, 1987, twelve days after my divorce from Jose was final, Dick and I were married despite my being an hour late for the wedding. Two days later, I became pregnant with my third and final child. Because I had a tendency toward premature labor, my doctor put me on complete bed rest for the last two months of my pregnancy. Dick's mother, Gail, came to lend a hand with my other children, and I loved having her there and since she was such a great help. But because she could only stay a month, Dick had to take care of us after she left. (I cried when she did.) He did a decent job but was not happy about it; I think he resented my not being able to take care of my responsibilities. Frankly, I wasn't thrilled about it either.

Finally, though, on January 22, 1988, I gave birth to RJ in San Diego. As usual for a mother, I thought he was the most perfect baby I had ever seen. I didn't want to bring him home because I knew if I did (or rather, when I did), I would have to share him with the neighborhood that I had become close to. All the ladies would want to hold him, and I cringed at the thought of giving him over to someone else. I didn't want him to be held by anyone but his immediate family. Dick really didn't have anything to do with him and never helped feed or change his diapers. But the ladies did eventually see him, and of course, they told me how gorgeous he was. I knew RJ would be the last child I would have because one week after his birth, I had a tubal ligation.

Despite being in a marriage that I didn't want, the first year I did try. After RJ's birth, the neighborhood children came to our house for a drink of Kool-Aid after playing outside on hot summer days. (At this time, I stopped drinking and attended church weekly. I tried my best to be a good mother and wife.) I always had at least four gallons of it in the refrigerator. This gave me an excellent opportunity to talk to them about Jesus. They would ask questions, and I'd tell them stories from the Bible to their willing ears. This turned into a weekly Bible study, and some of them accepted the Lord. One of those who did had previously stolen all of my children's Christmas presents. I forgave her, and we became very close. She ended up being my best student!

JJ was thrilled to be a big brother again, and Abigale just loved the idea of being a big sister. She would hold RJ in her little arms and tell everyone he was her baby. JJ was seven at the time of RJ's birth, and Abigale was two. She was very careful with him, always remembering to hold his head. Two weeks after RJ was born, JJ had me bring him and Abigale to his school for show-and-tell and did a wonderful job telling his classmates about them. He was very proud to be a brother of them.

Abigale had always been devoted to JJ and felt very possessive about him. When one young boy in our neighborhood made the mistake of calling JJ "his buddy" in front of Abigale, she hauled off and punched him in the mouth despite being only two and a half years old. Thankfully, we were friends with his parents, and they just laughed about it. I didn't scold her for it because at the time, I thought it was good that she was standing up for herself, something I had never been able to do.

I had many extramarital affairs while married to Dick. He had known, if I didn't marry him, and he decided he no longer wanted me and my children living with him, that I had no place else to go except back to Joan and Willie. And instead of helping me find other more acceptable living arrangements (that I'm sure existed but that I didn't know about), both he and Joan let me go through with a wedding I didn't really want but felt I had to for my children's sake. Consequently, the resentment I felt soon turned to hatred and disgust.

When he would come home from work and I had attended to all my "motherly" duties of making supper and putting the children to bed, I would then go to the Enlisted Men's Club and stay out all night drinking and having sex with the men I had met at the club until he left for work in the morning. He hated me doing this, but I would always tell him I didn't care about him, and what he wanted didn't matter to me. When I started attending college, Dick hired a nanny to stay with the children. She ended up being my biggest party buddy, along with several of the wives who lived around us. Like me, they were all cheating on their husbands too.

When Abigale was three, my father graduated from the college in Houston and wanted to continue his education at a college in California. Since we were living in military housing and had the room, Dick and I decided to let him stay with us. This turned out not to be good thing for my daughter because, unknown to me, he started molesting her.

After two months, I finally realized something was wrong with Abigale. I had noticed the signs of abuse but ignored them because I didn't think there was any reason for them. But one night, Abigale came running into my bedroom screaming, "There's a man in my room!" Immediately, I ran into her room and looked in all the possible places someone could hide. Of course, no one was there, and the thought that it had been my father never even entered my mind. When I went back to bed, Abigale went with me and spent the night wrapped in my arms.

The next morning, I took her across the street to a friend's house, thinking she wouldn't feel frightened away from our house. There I questioned her a few times about what happened, but at first, she wouldn't answer me. But then, after several minutes, she started crying and showed me where the man had touched her: on her private area.

That's when all the pieces fell into place. Abigale's reverting back into diaper even though before my father came, she was potty-trained; her not wanting to leave the house with me to go to the neighbor's because, she said, she and grandpa were "playing games"; and the fear in her eyes whenever I would ask her about it.

I was so furious, I stormed into our house and yelled at my dad to get his things and leave my home right now. He begged me to let him stay, saying he had no place else to go and, since he had only been in the area a few months, didn't know anyone else to stay with. I didn't care. I was not about to harbor someone who would harm any of my children, especially my daughter. Dick had called the police, and by the time they arrived, he was ready to leave. I was so angry at him that as they took him away, I told him that if I ever saw him on the street, I'd hit the gas instead of the brakes.

But with my anger came hurt that he would do such a thing. Never in a million years would I have thought my father, who had helped me so much in the past by taking me out of the foster care system that had failed me, would deliberately hurt someone I loved so much—and his own granddaughter! I remembered how he had treated us when I was very young, but I thought by now he had changed and deserved another chance. But I learned the hard way he hadn't. And he learned the hard way that my daughter was far more important to me than he was.

For several years after this incident, I made no effort to contact my father. But then, six months before he passed away, I started calling him weekly, encouraging him to exercise and go outside for walks. Through these phone calls, I read the Bible to him and told him how Jesus loved him and had died on the cross for him. I couldn't visit him to do this since he lived in Alvin, Texas, and I lived in Rochester, Minnesota. But as far as I know, he never repented of the evil he had committed to any of his family. He had been diagnosed with heart disease and died two years later in December 1998.

While still living with Dick in military housing, and before RJ's first birthday, I started attended college to earn an accounting degree. I loved it and made dean's List twice. However, Dick and I had literally begun fighting; he had started hitting me, and I had finally learned to hit back. It became so bad, I had to have him removed from the house and had a restraining order put on him. The Navy let me stay in the base housing a few weeks so I could find another place to live.

I found a two-bedroom apartment in Imperial Beach, and we moved into it, giving up on my marriage. RJ was ten months old, and because I was in school, we went on welfare. Without Dick around,

I was able to concentrate on my schooling, excelling in all my classes. My children and I would take trips to the beach several times a week. All of them loved the water, especially Abigale, whom we called our "fish." Without the constant arguments and fighting between Dick and me, life became much happier for all of us.

Despite the restraining order though, Dick still managed to harass me. Every day he would call and drive by our apartment. So it was a great relief when his ship went on a Westpac (a six-month cruise to far eastern countries, including Australia). I used the time to date several men. Still, it was a struggle for me to care for the children and go to college. Then, when Dick's ship returned, he had the vehicle I used for daily use (and that he was paying for) repossessed. Despite the fact that he had two other cars that were bought and payed for.

In order to receive the grant I had applied for, I had to have copies of some of the forms I had filled out, and Dick made them for me. I went to his office on the base because he said he could do it for free. But I forgot my address was on it, so he learned the physical address, because he knew where it was just not the address. After the car was repossessed, he would drive by often and made unannounced visits to the apartment.

A few weeks after I lost the car, Dick talked me into going into rehab for my alcohol abuse. (Though, for some reason, he didn't think he needed it despite drinking more each day than I did.) He also talked me into letting his mother Gail take all three of my children. We flew them up to Minnesota where she lived for what I thought would be a few months. However, she hadn't had them a month before retuning Abigale to her grandparents in Missouri, and returning JJ to Joan, all without my permission. Abigale's grandparents contacted Dick and let him know where she was, but Joan didn't bother to call. Gail kept RJ with her.

For the time Gail did have my other children, she didn't treat them with the same compassion she gave RJ. She practically abused Abigale, who was four at the time, by making her sleep in the dark when she was afraid and giving snacks to the other children but not her. She told her she was too fat to have any. She treated nine-year-old JJ better, but still not as well as she did RJ. The awful news come pouring in from grandma who now had Abigale.

I left the rehab center, and Dick came and picked me up. He rented us a one-bedroom apartment in a not-so-nice area of Spring Valley. There was a gang who controlled the area. Initially, with my children gone, I stayed in the apartment alone while Dick's ship went on its last Westpac. But then Peter, a neighbor's son, left his wife and came from Pennsylvania to live with them. After a few dates, I invited him to move in with me. He eventually became my third husband and my second longest marriage.

I wanted my children back, so Peter and I went to Ridgecrest to take to take JJ back from Joan. She was very upset since I had given her no warning that we were coming. Then I took a bus by myself from San Diego, California, to Winnona, Minnesota, to reclaim RJ. When I arrived at the house without warning, Gail wouldn't bring him out to me, so I had to call the police. She still wouldn't bring him out to me, so the police had to go to the door to get him. All she gave me for him were two outfits, his Bark Man (Bart Simpson) doll, and his quilt. On the bus ride back to California, RJ woke up crying about the monsters; he needed his doll and quilt for security. Unfortunately, somewhere along the way, the doll got left behind in a restaurant. When he realized it was gone, he was inconsolable, crying, and panicking. A sad event because he loved that doll.

While Dick was on Westpac he learned about Peter living with me, so he filed for divorce. At the time, I considered it was one of the happiest days of my life. (Had I known how it would end though, I wouldn't have.) I had just brought RJ and JJ back to be with me. (Abigale was still with her grandparents in Missouri), so Peter and I decided to move into a bigger apartment. This made Dick very angry and vindictive, since legally I was still his wife.

When Peter and I started living together in our own apartment, we decided to visit Joan and Izzy at Ridgecrest. (With Willie back in prison, I felt safe to visit.) This ended up being the last visit I would initiate. I really didn't want to go; I went mostly for JJ who loved his grandmother. We meant to stay the whole weekend with them, but the first day we were there, Joan started belittling me. She had told

Peter, "If you get tired of Karen, you can have Izzy." Both she and Izzy, sixteen at the time, thought this was funny. The next day, Izzy's first child, Joey, who was three, and RJ, who was four, were playing on the living room floor. While RJ was busy with a toy, Joey started hitting him for no reason, laughing as he did. Joan and Izzy encouraged him in this and joined in his laughter whenever he hit RJ. RJ told Joey to stop every time he hit him, but the last hit was so hard, he started crying. When I went to slap at Joey's hand to discipline him, Joan jumped up and told me to get out of her house.

I was so angry, I just headed for the bedroom where our things were and started packing. In my anger, when I yanked the closet door open, it fell off the track. (Trailer houses aren't very well built.) When Joan heard the crash, she ran into the room, and seeing me bent over to pick up our bags, she grabbed and pulled me by my hair. Without thinking, I reached up and hit her. That produced an outburst of indignation, yelling at me not to hit her and not to tear up her house. Izzy had come to the door and added to the melee by yelling at me not to hit her mother. At the same time, Peter came in and tackled me on to the bed. Joan left taking Izzy with her, and within a few minutes, we had our belongings in the car and were headed back to San Diego.

Divorce proceedings from Dick had started by this time and my life, as far as my children were concerned, went from bad to worse. Because he had accused me of taking drugs, he was to have paid for three drug tests; he paid for none of them. I paid for the only one to prove I wasn't on drugs. I had cleaned up and had even started attending church again with Peter. His claim took precedence though, and the court gave him temporary custody of RJ. I was to have visitation rights, but Dick denied them to me for all but a few visits (his mother had come from Minnesota to help). The court eventually gave Dick permanent custody, but since he had recently been transferred to Italy and would be leaving soon, they told him he was not to take RJ out of the country. (After the divorce was final, he ignored this order and took him out of the country anyway.)

Our divorce was final on May 19, 1992. The last time I saw my four-year-old son, he called me a whore. I left crying, not understanding why he would say that. (I realize now that someone had told him to say that.) My family—Peter, JJ, Abigale's grandparents and my fellow church members—continued to support me regardless of the court's decision. Because Dick defied the court by taking RJ to Italy with him, it would be twenty years later before I saw him again.

We had a mediator for our divorce, and he had asked Joan her opinion of letting me keep RJ. She told him she thought it would be better for the boy if his father had custody of him so he could live with his grandparents in Minnesota while Dick was on active duty. She then asked that she be given custody of JJ (Abigale was already with her grandparents in Missouri.) She went on to say that I was not a good mother and didn't think I deserved to have custody of *any* of my children because I was a drunk and irresponsible. At the hearing, the mediator read to the court what Joan had said. (At the time, it seemed funny to me that *she* would condemn *my* mothering skills!)

Because Joan never seemed to support me in anything I did or wanted to do, I've always thought she still held against me my accusations of abuse by her and Willie. Though she had to know they were true, to acknowledge them would be to prove me right and her wrong, and I don't think she could ever handle that. So she has tried to hurt me any way she can and, unfortunately, has succeeded more than once. Having RJ taken from me was one of those times. I hope I would never hurt any of my children as she has hurt me.

The main reason I lost RJ was an incident that happened when he was two years old. The children had gotten up early one fall day and were playing in the living room in our second-story apartment. Dick had had overnight guard duty and hadn't returned home yet, and, unfortunately, I had been drinking the night before and was still asleep. RJ started running on the top of the back of the couch that was against one of the windows and lost his balance and fell out onto the concrete sidewalk just below us. JJ and Abigale immediately woke me and told me what had happened. I was so shaken, it took me a few minutes to get dressed, just grabbing anything I could find. (As I did, I remember yelling, "Why didn't you stop him?" as if it was their fault. That comment still haunts me today, and I've always regretted saying it, especially since I don't think I ever told them I was sorry for blaming them.)

As I went down the stairs to see if he was still alive, I saw that my friend, Erica, who had spent the night, had already gone to RJ and had told him that "his mommy" would be down soon. Thankfully, he was conscious and asking for me. When I saw him, I was so terrified of what I would find that I couldn't go near him, so Erica stayed with him until the ambulance came. (Our roommate Ken had called them as soon as the accident had happened.) After he was carefully placed on a gurney and loaded into the vehicle, I climbed in to ride to the hospital with him. Along the way, the medics asked questions as to how the incident happened that I couldn't answer. I kept telling them I had been asleep and didn't know any of the details. From their reactions, I think they thought I was lying. Shaking and crying at the thought of losing my child, I asked if he would be all right. "I don't know" was the only answer I received.

At the hospital, the nurses were more kind. At the hospital, RJ was rushed into X-ray to find out what kind of injuries he had sustained. They found that he had a concussion and a few scrapes on his head that they had cleaned and bandaged with gauze. The nurses informed me that RJ would have to stay in the hospital overnight for observation. I spent the rest of the day and all night there, going home only to eat and change my clothes. Our roommate and Erica watched JJ and Abigale until Dick returned home after dark. I slept on the small couch in the waiting room, waking up several times to check on RJ. Thankfully, I usually found him sleeping soundly.

The next morning, after the doctor examined him again, he was released. When one of the nurses told me he would be okay but would be sore for a few weeks, I was greatly relieved. She explained to me that children are more resilient than adults and that he would recover just fine. (To this day, RJ is doing just fine) Despite this good news, however, when I returned home with RJ, Dick became very angry at me and blamed me for the accident; it was my fault for not watching him and making him mind. I don't know why he thought he needed to chastise me; I felt guilty enough as it was.

When the verdict on the custody hearing was given, Dick had custody of RJ; I could only have him on holidays, and then only with supervised visits. The thought of not being able to have my baby totally devastated me and made my heartache so intense that as I walked out of the courtroom, I fell to the floor sobbing. The lady security guard helped me up and took me to the restroom, where she helped me clean my face. When we came out, I saw Dick. I glared at him and said, "As God as my witness, you will regret this day!" The security guard pulled me away from him but not before I saw him laugh at me. (But I ended up having the last laugh; RJ doesn't have any contact with him now.)

Though I prayed often for God to bring RJ back to me, it never happened. Instead, I've had to live with the pain of not being able to raise my youngest child. Dick knew I didn't love him and knew how devastated I would be at losing RJ, but he didn't care. From his point of view, I had hurt him (Abigale was already with her grandparents in Missouri), or he was going to hurt me. For weeks after the hearing, all I did was stay in bed and cry. JJ was the only child I had with me, and I was thankful for his presence. He and Peter stood by me and did their best to comfort me until I could function again.

When I had finally at least partially recovered from having RJ taken away, Peter, JJ, and I moved to Poplar Bluff, Missouri, in the first part of 1992, where Abigale lived with her grandparents. Our car had needed a new transmission, and Peter and JJ had put it in. They must have done a pretty good job because we traveled all the way from San Diego, California, a distance of 1,800 miles, to Poplar Bluff, Missouri, with no problems. A miracle! The differences between Southern California and Southern Missouri were huge, and it took some time for me to get used to the changes. But the natural beauty of my new home state, plus the love and support from God and Abigale's grandmother helped me heal from losing my son. Grandma had always been like a mother to me, helping me by her love and compassion and the wisdom she shares from God's Word.

In 2011, Abigale found RJ on Facebook. He was twenty-two, living in the Twin Cities in Minnesota going to college. I was very excited! Abigale and JJ, who had been keeping in contact with him through Facebook, invited him to come down to see us, JJ, and Abigale as well as me. Though he was glad to see his siblings and very proud to be an uncle, he and I really didn't get along. I think part of the reason was because my lifestyle at the time wasn't the greatest. I was drinking daily and having friends over to party at my apartment preferring that to spending time with him. I also feared Dick would once again come between us, so the anger I had toward his father intensified, and I'm sure he could see it. I've asked RJ for another chance, since I truly felt I mistreated him during that first visit. I didn't want to spend time with him; all I cared about was drinking at the time. He has since forgiven me, and our relationship is doing fine.

CHAPTER TWELVE

❖❖❖   ❖❖❖   ❖❖❖   ❖❖❖

Peter

MOVING TO MISSOURI BECAME THE most important move of my life. Peter and I married on November 27, 1992, with Grandma (Abigale's grandmother) performing the ceremony in the church where she was the assistant pastor. Grandpa, her husband, made the most beautiful wedding cake I'd ever seen. His experience came from having been a cook in the army. All four of us settled nicely into the Midwest country living, and for once, we started having a normal life. Grandma became a very influential part of that life, finally giving me an older woman I could look up to. Both she and Grandpa loved JJ as if he were their own, and of course, they spoiled Abigale as much as they could. I attended her church, eventually becoming the Sunday school teacher for the children. We all went as a family, at least twice a week.

A few weeks after we arrived at Poplar Bluff, Peter found a job hanging gutter and siding. He loved the work so much that he eventually, with a partner, opened his own business. It did so well that we bought a used trailer and started remodeling it. We had continued attending church as a family at least two times a week. But then everything started falling apart.

The problems started about a year after moving to Missouri, about the time Peter started his own business. Our first separation was during this time. Peter began staying gone for days at a time. I wouldn't eat and could sleep only a few hours a night. He would leave and not say anything about where he was going or when he would be back or who he was with. We ended up being separated several times, but then we would always manage to work things out. Even though I forgave him, the trust I had in him was gone out of our marriage.

Whenever Peter was home, I noticed his behavior had changed drastically. He didn't care about his business or working during this time, and he was spending a lot of money, but not helping with the bills. When I asked him what was wrong, he wouldn't talk to me about it; all he wanted to do was argue and fight. I recognized all the signs of drug abuse, but I chose to ignore them. I did talk with Grandma about it, but she never had to deal with this kind of situation, so she couldn't give me advice or sympathize with me. The only good thing was that I had quit drinking and smoking for two years while this was going on.

Because of Peter's changed behavior, his business eventually failed. I told my sister Brenda about it, and she suggested we move to Rochester, Minnesota, where she lived. She said it was a great place to live, and there were plenty of jobs. So in the summer of 1996, we took a trip to see her and Rochester. She was right; it was a beautiful town. On the return trip, Peter and I discussed it and decided to take a chance on the move. Abigale and I went first, and Peter and JJ followed a few months later. Peter started going to church with us again and leaving the house for unknown periods of time. I assumed he had gotten off the drugs, but I still didn't trust him. If anything happened though, I would have my family to help me.

About a month after we arrived, we rented a large attractive house within the city limits. My sister had been kind enough to let us stay with her family until finding a place of our own. Abigale was ten when we left, soon to be eleven. Abigale was going into the sixth grade, and JJ was a sophomore in high school. Their cousins were fellow schoolmates. I wanted this move to be as comfortable for my children as possible and made being with family a priority since I didn't have that luxury when I was growing up. As a result, my niece and nephews became quite close to Abigale and JJ, and because I was able to spend as much time as I wanted with my sister (whom I had always admired), our relationship flourished as well.

While living in Minnesota, Peter and I did really well financially. Our bills were always paid on time, with enough leftover each month we could splurge a little. This enabled Abigale and me to spend much needed quality time together shopping clothes. We were able to purchase nice vehicles, a king cab truck for Peter and a sports car for me, though both were slightly used. Peter's siding business was doing very well, and I found work at a debt collection company and then later for Mayo Clinic posting payments.

After eight years of marriage, we purchased a double-wide trailer house on a contract for deed. It was the most beautiful house I had ever seen. It had a fireplace, two small bedrooms and the master bedroom, two baths, a den, and a large formal living room. I especially loved the large and spacious kitchen. Though our beautiful new home was situated in an upscale trailer park, JJ and Abigale would still jokingly call us "trailer trash." We would laugh about it.

Despite all this improvement to our material lives, our marriage once again started faltering. Peter's drug use became worse. Looking back, I was very insecure and jealous of him; stability was important to me because of my children. Maybe I ask too much of him to be a good father to JJ and Abigale, without him being their real father. Whatever the cause, Peter came to me in February 1999, after almost nine years of marriage, wanting a divorce. He didn't give me a reason or a choice. It was his decision, and I had no say in the matter. I tried desperately to talk him out of it, but he wouldn't change his mind. I called Grandma the next day and asked if Abigale and I could stay with her until we could make other arrangements. She agreed and wanted details about when we would arrive. JJ stayed with Peter in our home until he graduated high school a few months later. With him being seventeen, I gave him the choice of what he wanted to do.

Shocked and horrified, I stayed for one week before taking Abigale and moving back to her grandmother's in Poplar Bluff. We stayed with her for six months before moving into low-income housing. For nearly a year, I couldn't talk about Peter without crying. We ended up staying with her for six months before moving into low-income housing. For nearly a year, I couldn't talk about Peter without crying. We had been together for almost eleven years, two living together, and nine married, and I thought I had finally found the man I would spend the rest of my life with. It totally devastated me.

It was especially hard for me since living in Poplar Bluff again, I saw many things that reminded me of Peter and the good times we had together. Thankfully, though, I found a job almost immediately as a waitress in a restaurant. When Abigale and I moved into low-income housing, we didn't have much to put into it, but it was ours. And even though I didn't want anyone full-time in my life, I did start dating again. Gradually, my heart began to heal from the break with Peter, with the reality that we would never be together again finally sinking in. Our divorce that I never contested was final on October 23, 2000.

Abigale and I had returned to the church we had previously attended, and that I loved and missed. The pastor and his wife supported me, and they, as well as my church friends—both new and old—helped me heal from the heartbreak I had experienced. (At this time, Grandma didn't have her own church.) For several months, I seriously focused on God and the Bible, attending services with my daughter. But then, the loneliness and insecurity I had always had and the immorality of my life overwhelmed my soul. I left these people and once again drifted away from the teachings of Jesus in order to the ways of the world. Abigale and Grandma would ask me why I wasn't going to church any longer, but I would ignore the question.

CHAPTER THIRTEEN

❖❖❖ ❖❖❖ ❖❖❖ ❖❖❖

Jack

JACK CAME INTO MY LIFE through my involvement with another man. I had dated Robert a few times, and he had what seemed to me a very obnoxious friend named Jack whom I couldn't stand. He kept making unwanted comments to me like, "Take me home with you, and I'll show you a good time!" Or he would go on and on about how beautiful I was. He creeped me out because he was always around, almost like he was following me. Robert had told him that I loved to go dancing on ladies' night at a local bar, so Jack made sure he was always there. Robert lived just blocks from my house and drove the same road I would. Jack was always with him, so I would see him a few times a week. He always called me Cookies, a nickname my friends and I had for marijuana.

However, despite these initial feelings, however, over time Jack managed to finagle his way into my life and then into my heart. He accomplished this gradually by doing little things like striking up petty conversation with me at the local bar that, at first, I would walk away from him. But then, he began to make me laugh. He also turned on the charm by always complimenting me, making me feel pretty whenever I was around him. After about two months of him not being obnoxious, I actually started to like him. Though he had stopped asking me to take him home, one night I did. I was thirty-eight, and he was thirty. I then met his mother and daughter and instantly fell in love with both of them. (I actually liked them more than I did him. Eventually, though, for some reason, I can't remember his mother, and I had a falling out, and we never spoke again.)

On October 16, 2002, I married Jack, my fourth husband, at the Missouri state prison, in Charleston, Missouri, where he was doing time for robbery. Unfortunately, Jack had hidden his true self until after I had married him. After he was released and living at home with me, he became demanding and controlling. The charm was no longer there.

As you can imagine, our relationship didn't last very long. I guess I had been around worldly, abusive men so long that I found the "bad boy" persona attractive. As with most of my other husbands, Jack could be very loving when he had his way but would start yelling and being aggressive toward me when he didn't. He reminded me of my father. We frequently argued, and he was constantly in and out of prison. When he wasn't in prison, he wouldn't work, supporting himself—and sometimes us—by stealing. Abigale lived with us and had never liked him; I should have taken her cue. I finally divorced him after about a year of marriage. I filed for divorce twice but stopped the first time. The second time, though, I let it go through.

The first time I filed, Jack had been incarcerated again for stealing, and I and Abigale, who was fourteen at the time, had moved to Kansas City with two of his woman friends. We went there because Jack wanted to live in Kansas City after he was released. He said that he trusted these young women to help Abigale and me. We moved into the apartment that the two women had already rented, and each of us was supposed to pitch in to help pay for food, rent, and other bills. But after two months, this arrangement fell apart. One of the women wouldn't work and, therefore, couldn't and wouldn't help pay for anything. Though I had found work at a steakhouse, making good money in tips, I had a daughter to support and couldn't carry both my and her obligations.

I finally gave up and moved back to Poplar Bluff where I had an affair with one of my ex-boyfriends. I missed the touch of a man, and he was kind and gentle to me. Though this was the only time I cheated on Jack, I felt guilty enough that when I went to see him one weekend, I told him about it. He was so mad, he called me every foul name he could think of, yelling so loud the whole visitation room could hear him. Totally embarrassed, I just walked out and a few days later filed for divorce. This was the first time I filed, and Jack talked me out of it in a letter by telling me he was sorry for the way he treated me and would never talk to me that way again.

The second time I filed, Jack had been released from prison and was living with me and Abigale in the trailer I had bought on contract for deed from Grandma. I was an office manager at a car lot in town, and it had taken us six months to get back on our feet after Kansas City. JJ had moved back from Minnesota and also lived with us. (Peter lost the double-wide, had gotten a job, and rented an apartment with a roommate. He had let JJ stay with him until he had graduated from high school.) Though JJ was nineteen, Jack thought he needed to tell him what to do, making rules he had to follow. I didn't mind some of them, but some were for a young child. Like helping with housework, which he already did, but Jack felt like he had to tell him that. One evening, JJ became angry at Jack for some reason that I can't remember why and walked into town. He was arrested for loitering and came home when he was released a few days later. I had no idea he had been arrested and had worried about his whereabouts the few days he was gone. He moved out, and that's when I decided I'd had enough of Jack. I again filed for divorce, giving him the choice of the house or the car. He chose the house. A month later, I had the electricity shut off, and he had to move back in with his mother. Abigale and I moved back into the trailer. Jack was very evasive about being served the papers. It didn't take long before he was back in prison, and that's when he finally received them. We were officially divorced on April 1, 2004. I called our relationship the April fool's marriage.

CHAPTER FOURTEEN

◇◇◇   ◇◇◇   ◇◇◇   ◇◇◇

George

SHORTLY BEFORE DIVORCING JACK, I met my fifth and final husband. In January 2004, one of my acquaintances, who was dating a man I was also dating, strongly urged me to meet George one Friday night. (I suspect she wanted to get me away from our mutual boyfriend.) I told her I had another engagement, so I wouldn't be able to stay long. But after meeting George, I decided to cancel my other date, and we, along with his boss, went to a bar where we spent the evening getting to know each other. We played darts, feeling sorry for me because he kept beating me. We laughed and talked about our jobs. The whole evening, he was a gentleman.

For almost nine months, George and I dated, but the relationship was very one-sided. He was twenty-eight and had been single for a long time, I don't think he was ready for a full-time girlfriend. He wasn't mean, just didn't apply his heart to the relationship like I did. He lived in Doniphan (a smaller town about twenty-five miles west of Poplar Bluff) and was a steady and reliable worker. He was also very handsome, and most of the local Doniphan girls were extremely jealous that I, an outsider from Poplar Bluff, had captivated the town's most eligible bachelor. They showed me their jealousy by giving me dirty looks and ignoring me whenever I was around them, trying to entice George to sleep with them, and generally let me know I was not wanted. I just ignored them whenever I could.

The business I worked at was closing the doors, so I applied for several jobs in both Poplar Bluff and Doniphan; the one in Doniphan hired me. Since the trailer I had bought from Grandma and was living in needed major repairs, I asked George if I could move in with him. He said yes and also that he would help me financially as much as he could. Thus began a relationship that started out pretty rocky but would, through major life-changing events that had yet to occur, smooth out and become the best one I ever had.

At the time I met George, he had a roommate living with him. When I moved in, unknown to me, the roommate started telling tales to George about what supposedly went on between us when George was gone. He reacted by not coming home at night and not telling me where he was. But then, he got fed up with that and asked me to move out. Without questioning him, I did and rented a house in Doniphan. When I went back to George's to pick up what I had left behind, his roommate answered the door. When I told him why I was there, he said he'd bring my things to me so we could spend some time together. I bluntly told him that I didn't want to be with him, didn't want to hang out with him, and didn't want to have anything to do with him! I later learned from George that his roommate's lies were the reason he had acted the way he had toward me. When I confronted this person about it, he denied ever saying anything like that to anyone. Then he asked, "Who he was supposed to have told?" George, standing right there with us, looked right at him and said, "Me."

While living in this cute little house in Doniphan, my boss started flirting with me. He had helped me get the house by giving me the first and last month's rent, as well as the deposit. Though I was making weekly payments to pay him back, I guess he thought I owed him something because the flirting intensified. When I refused his advances, he retaliated by accusing me of taking money from the business. I put up with this as long as I could, but finally had to quit, finding another job almost immediately.

Since George thought I had been unfaithful to him, he decided he was free to go with anyone he wanted, so he started spending time with one of the local girls. While he was at my house one night, she actually came to my door and asked for him to go with her. He felt so bad, he never voluntarily came over after that. I still wanted him in my life though, so later, about a week and a half, I went to his house to talk with him. He confessed he preferred to be with me. So we tried again.

When we first started our relationship, it became painfully obvious that most of George's friends did not want us together. Some belittled him, and others wanted him to spend more time with them than me. The friends he had used him because of his knowledge of small engines. He was always going to fix something for someone; his friends made sure of it. They were primarily responsible for most of our breakups and separations before and after we married. Thankfully, though, it's not that way today after twelve years of marriage. George has learned to recognize their destructive behavior and doesn't let it come between us. His real friends are becoming closer, while those who try to manipulate him have become less a part of our lives.

After talking with George and realizing he still loved me, he eventually moved into the little house with me. One night, while he was talking with his sister on the phone, I overheard him tell her that he was getting married. Slightly hurt, I asked him, "Who are you marrying?" He grinned from ear to ear and said, "You." What a way to propose! Our wedding took place at the courthouse on October 14, 2004.

I might have had a different husband, but I still hadn't changed. On Friday, a few months after we were married, I told George that I wanted to go see a local band I liked and knew as friends and asked if he wanted to go. He told me no, answering me in a way that made me feel like I was a bother to him. So I asked a friend of mine if she wanted to go, and she said yes.

So that evening while George stayed with my friend's husband at their house, she and I went to watch the band. However, being a lifelong alcoholic plus being depressed over the way George had treated me earlier, I had been drinking all day and was rather drunk by the time we arrived at the dumpy bar in a town nearby where the band usually played. A few hours later, our husbands showed up (I believe to check up on us.) I went to the bathroom a few minutes after they arrived, then started to talk with one of the guys in the band. I was still upset with George, so when the band member asked me if I wanted to have a drink with him from a bottle of whiskey he wanted me to try, I agreed.

So I went outside to his truck and had one drink with him. The whiskey was very strong, and having that drink was one of the last things I remember. The drink was very strong, but I do remember not having sex with him. As drunk as I have gotten, that's the one thing I can remember. I became so drunk that I couldn't walk, and my friend left me in his truck, telling me he would take me home when he was done playing. However, he had left the keys behind, and in my drunken haze, I must have thought I could drive myself home because the next thing I remember was seeing headlights coming at me.

Realizing what I had done (but still quite drunk), I tried to turn the truck around by pulling into somebody's driveway. Unfortunately, I didn't realize it still had the medium-sized trailer the band used to carry all their equipment, so when I turned around, I ran over a Jon boat. The owners of the house came running out, then called the cops on me. (I still don't remember driving away from the bar.)

I was arrested that night and spent the next six days in jail. Consequently, I lost my job. George told me he wouldn't come and bail me out until Friday because he thought I had been unfaithful to him. (In a way, I was and have constantly regretted walking out that door.) However, I called Grandma and Abigale, and they came and bailed me out on Thursday since I had to be held for seventy-two hours before I could see a judge to get my bond set. That didn't happen until Wednesday. Abigale took me back to my house, and George was still there. Though I was hurt by his response to my arrest, I was still afraid of his reaction when I came home because I knew I had hurt him badly. I hadn't expected to see him when I arrived. However, he told me he didn't love me anymore and moved out the next day. We were apart for almost a year, the longest separation I had to endure through our entire marriage.

Part of the reason for our separations stemmed from misunderstandings between what I told George and what friends told him about various things that happened when he wasn't around. One good example was an incident that occurred a few months after we had gotten back together after my arrest. I had gone with my friend (the one who had been with me when I was arrested) to a bar in a town about twenty miles from Doniphan. While there, I had started talking with a woman I had known for several years. Then I went to the bathroom. By the time I came out, I couldn't find my friend, but her truck was still in the parking lot, so I figured I'd wait for her there. Well, about forty-five minutes later, I had to use the restroom again. (People who drink a lot of beer spend a lot of time in bathrooms.) When I came back out to the parking lot, both she and the truck were gone. She later told George that she couldn't find me and thought I had left with someone else. Of course, George thought that someone else was a man, and he chose to believe my friend rather than me.

Though George and I remained married, we lived apart more than we lived together for the first eight and a half years of our marriage. I believe his friends coming between us and my insecurity were the primary cause of our separations. Not being able to communicate and trust each other with our feelings was a big problem for both of us. But then, the call came from San Marcos, asking me to appear at Willie Roy Jenkins's sentencing trial, and he was the only one who would go with me. In fact, he didn't even have to think about it; he agreed immediately. That told me a lot about how he felt about me. Despite this, though, we didn't say much to each other during the two-day trip to Texas, but I think part of it was because he just didn't know what to say to me. He knew my testimony would be a major event in my life, but because I had never shared that part of my past with him, he just didn't know how major.

After the trial, the PTSD hit me so badly that George took me back to live with him, and we've been together ever since. Now that he knows what I had been through as a child, he took care of me like a true husband, enduring the difficulties of dealing with my psychological problems brought on by having to relive my past. He made sure I went to my doctor's appointments, and that I had—and took—my medicine. A new understanding developed between us, and now we love each other even with all our faults, a love that grows ever stronger with each passing day. I've become a homebody, and George, always hard-working and dependable, has become the best husband I ever had. He still spends time with his friends, but now he's become very selective, only encouraging friendships with those we both like and can get along with. I am forever thankful to God that He brought George into my life—and kept him there throughout all our trials and tribulations.

CHAPTER FIFTEEN

❖❖ ❖❖ ❖❖ ❖❖

Four Good Guys (Not All Men Are Bad)

IN CASE YOU'VE REACHED THIS point in my story and think that all the men I ever knew had mistreated me, I've dedicated this chapter to the four really compassionate and caring ones who helped me through their devoted friendships. Out of respect for their current relationships and not wanting to cause anyone problems, I've changed all their names except one.

Darren

I met Darren in 1989 while still married to Dick and living in San Diego. He also was in the Navy. I don't recall how we met, but we quickly became good friends. He often visited the house Dick and I shared, along with other friends of ours. He genuinely cared about how I felt and what I said. No man had ever treated me like that. He paid attention to my moods and body language so well that he could tell immediately whenever anything was bothering me. Then he'd want to know what it was, would listen intently to what I told him, then offer feedback and advice about how to deal with it. Then, to make me feel better, he'd start acting silly until I laughed. It usually worked. As a result, every time I was with Darren, whether sitting at home or playing pool at a local bar, just being around him with his laughter and sweet words always made my day wonderful.

Darren nicknamed me Biscuit, explaining that he and an old friend used that name for any pretty women. He often told me I was perfect and beautiful, and this nickname reminded me of that. Our relationship eventually grew to the point that we became lovers. I felt no qualms about cheating on Dick since his reasons for wanting me to marry him were only for his convenience, not mine. Even if Dick were around, Darren and I would talk between ourselves, ignoring him. Dick would get angry but never reprimanded me. One of our favorite things to do was taking trips to the beach, sometimes all three of us, and other times just Darren and me. I once sunburned so badly, I very carefully had to get back into my shorts and T-shirt; Darren was the one who helped me.

Shortly before leaving on Westpac (the same one that Dick had to leave on), we were sitting in a small building that had vending machines, tables, and a jukebox on the beach, on the naval base. Darren played the song "Fly to the Angels" by Slaughter, which was our favorite song, and Darren played it about ten times; I cried while listening to it knowing I would not be seeing him for at least six months. I still think about him whenever I hear that song.

It broke my heart when he finally left (unlike Dick whom I was glad to see leave.) While Darren was gone, I sent him goodie packages and "talked" to him through recorded cassette tapes. He's send me tapes of him playing "Say What You Will" by Fastway (a song I used to dance to when I danced topless.) Along with words of encouragement and humor, he'd also tell me about what he did overseas and how beautiful each port was. I'll forever be thankful for the way he always made me feel special and loved, never showing jealousy about anything I did or anyone I associated with.

While on Westpac, Darren decided to end our relationship. He said he didn't want to be in a long-term commitment. My divorce from Dick was in its final stages, and Darren's decision really broke my heart as I had thought that maybe we could marry when he returned. Peter was to take care of me while Darren was gone to sea, a deal that they had made with each other. I would much rather have married Darren than Peter, but then, I might not have met the other "good guys" in my life.

Ronnie

Ronnie worked late nights at one of the Poplar Bluff radio stations, playing song request from listeners, and it was through this that I initially "met" him. My friend Susie and I would call and request songs while we were drinking at her house, and he would always play what we asked for. The first time I talked to him, he made me laugh hysterically. (Being able to make me laugh is one of the most important qualities I look for in a man.) He was thirty-one, and I was thirty-seven when we met in 2000.

I started having long conversations with him a few days after that initial call. I'd call every night, and our talks would last into the early morning hours. We didn't actually meet face-to-face though until about two weeks later. He had mentioned he had a night off coming up, and we agreed to meet at a nearby fast-food place in the park. Having never seen a picture of him, I didn't realize how truly handsome he was with beautiful long brown hair and smiling eyes. I was a little leery of meeting him at first because he had asked Susie what I looked like. She told him I was pretty, with long hair and a big butt, but that hadn't been the description I had given him, and I was afraid he would think that one of us had lied. But, obviously, it didn't matter to him because our late-night talks developed into a closer relationship.

Working full-time during the day, then spending hours talking with Ronnie at night, gave me three or four hours to sleep. But it was worth it. He constantly made me laugh with his witty sense of humor. He knew a lot about music, and it was our mutual love of classic rock that brought us together.

Ronnie's popularity had started to grow in Poplar Bluff, so sometimes he would do live broadcasts at one of the local businesses during the day. He'd bring donuts for the employees, and if there were any left by the end of the broadcast, he'd stop by where I worked and leave them for me and my fellow workers. I remember him doing this twice, and it made a good impression on my bosses. Like me, they thought he was a very special guy.

On top of everything else, Ronnie was also a great cook. He made spaghetti for us one evening, and it was the best spaghetti I had ever eaten. Since I was not used to having a meal prepared for me by a man, I found it very romantic; I greatly enjoyed our evening together.

When we first started dating, Ronnie's popularity as a local celebrity had started to rise. We had gone to a bar one night, and the DJ there who had worked with Ronnie announced that he was in the building. Of course, the spotlight focused on him, and not wanting that same attention on me, I tried to hide behind him. His celebrity status sometimes made me uncomfortable, but I knew it was part of his job.

We enjoyed spending time together, with neither of us being bothered by our showing affection for each other in public. Ronnie was always considerate when he spoke to me and treated my daughter Abigale with the same respect, something none of my other boyfriends had ever done. Consequently, she also enjoyed being around him. I loved that he treated Abigale so well. She and Ronnie's sister used to say we should have married.

The business where I worked was moving to Memphis, and they wanted me to go with them, but because of the cost of living down there, I declined. We had been together for six months by this time, so I also didn't want to leave Ronnie. Despite this though, at a party at his sister's house one weekend, I had drunk too much and had made a complete fool of myself by trying to hook him up with another girl I knew he wasn't attracted to. We fought all that night about it because I was drunk. I cried. The thought of leaving him alone hurt me to the core.

Until recently, his sister and I had been very close friends. After returning from testifying, the rage I felt spilt over to everyone. When I spent the three days at my cabin drinking, I tried to call her, but she didn't answer. Not realizing she was at work, I left a mean message on her phone. The last time I saw her was at her work. She told me she had been at work and couldn't answer her phone and asked why I was being mean to her. She said that I had hurt her feelings. But because I was so full of anger, her confronting me infuriated me, and I left. We liked each other and had gotten along well from our first meeting. My being close to Ronnie's family and he being close to my daughter made our relationship easier; family interference was one problem neither of us had to worry about.

My relationship with Ronnie was my first serious one after my third husband Peter one year and a half years after leaving Minnesota. But because I was a heavy drinker, and a bit of a drama queen that caused me to make bad decisions while drunk, he wouldn't commit to me. After six months, that behavior was what broke us up. I will always regret acting that way. I call myself his "in-between wives, girlfriend" because we did date two more times, between his first and second wives, and then again between his second and third wives. But I always enjoyed going with him; Ronnie always gave me a good time. He was the only one who was not a musician in this group of "good guys."

Brent

I met Brent through old friends. Most of the people I hung around with at the time were musicians and their girlfriends or wives. I had seen him at their houses a few times but was dating Ronnie. His smile, soft-spoken voice, and beautiful black hair that fell midway down his back was very attractive. He was a large man, tall and muscular, who looked intimidating to those who didn't know him. But I discovered he was just a big teddy bear with the kindest and sweetest heart of any man I had known and wouldn't hurt anyone. I always felt safe and protected around him though.

The lead guitarist of a local band, Brent helped me forget Ronnie. Though I could tell he really didn't want a steady girlfriend, I grew on him. He had invited me to be with him to one of the band's gig (performances), and on the way home, I became so sleepy,

I laid my head on his lap without asking. I mark this as the beginning of our serious relationship.

I met Brent after Abigale and I had been living in low-income housing for about a year. He would stay with us over the weekends, and we'd party like we were rock stars. As his band was becoming more popular, we spent more time at bars watching him play. I always felt so proud to be seen with him, and he would make it clear to all his lady fans that he was already spoken of. Even though these women would go crazy over him, I couldn't get jealous because I knew, when the evening was over, he'd be leaving with me.

Brent would try to make me smile even when I wasn't feeling well. Once, when I was sick to my stomach, he told me to hold my finger on a certain spot on the neck of his guitar. He strummed the strings and, smiling, told me, "You just played a G." I grinned as if I'd done something spectacular. He would also put me before the other members of the band. Whenever we'd ride in Brent's van to a gig, he'd ask everyone what CD they wanted to listen to. I'd yell out the name of my favorite group, and all the others would moan, "Ahhhh, not again!" Brent would still put it in first; it seemed that making me happy was the biggest goal of his day.

I was the most sociable of the bands' four wives and girlfriends. I would talk to as many people at the bar as I could and party with them, getting up and dancing with the customers, then inviting them to come sit at "the band table" to have drinks and talk with me. Brent often told me he liked me to do this since it was great publicity. He even created a website for the group and posted pictures I had taken of their performances as well as some of their fans. The band had a CD out, and we had planned to send it to some bars in Memphis where there would be more exposure and more pay for their performances.

However, one of the wives didn't like him doing either of these things because she thought she needed to have full control of everything. So she called a meeting, inviting everyone but Brent. They decided she would be the only one to handle all their advertising. (This did more harm than good, eventually causing the band to break up.) Brent didn't appreciate not being included in this decision, so he quit and started a new band.

We lived together at two different times in our relationship. The first time, we rented a beautiful house in Poplar Bluff. Both of us worked for the same company; I was the secretary, and he was part of the crew. As a result, he was gone a lot, and I became lonely, causing me to make decisions that I would seriously regret later on. Jack had contacted me by phone while he was in prison, wanting me to marry him. I agreed. Though to this day, I could not tell you why. I knew Brent wanted to marry me but had not yet got around to asking me. So I went ahead and married Jack.

But when I finally realized what a huge mistake I had made and filed for divorce the first time, I went back to Brent. Technically, though, since I was still married, I was having an affair. Surprisingly, this made me feel guilty enough I told Jack while he was still in prison. As I said above, he didn't think too much of my confession. When I told Brent what happened, he responded, "At least you slept with someone who cares about you." It didn't help much, but it was sweet of him to say it.

The second time we lived together, we stayed in the trailer I had bought. But because I had gone out with one of his friends while we were living together, there were hard feeling between us. I knew I had hurt him, and though I felt lousy about it, I never apologized. Once again, because of my poor self-image and self-hatred and unfaithful behavior, I pushed away a man who would have been good for me.

But because of my disloyal behavior toward him, he once wrote a hateful song about me. I don't blame him after the totally unfair way I treated him. His huge loving heart eventually forgave me though, and today, we're once again friends. He has no knowledge of Willie or the PTSD. He eventually found and married another woman from Poplar Bluff and had remained with her through everything. I consider her very blessed to have him.

John

The last good guy was also part of a band, and I met him at a bar where he was playing. My best friend at the time worked at this bar and had invited me to see and hear his group, bragging about how good they were. George and I had separated again in 2011 after a huge argument, and I hadn't wanted to do anything except work and go home. I really didn't want to go see the group, but because she had invited me, I decided to anyway.

My friend was right though: the band was very good. As she and I were dancing on the dance floor to their music, she caught my eye and motioned for me to turn around. I did and saw one of the guitar players intently gazing at me, with his guitar pointed right at me. It was John, and this made me nervous because he was very young, not even out of his teen years.

After we danced and the band members were taking a break, we sat at the same table as John. He became angry when he learned that the girl he was going with was fooling around with another boy and slammed his soda down on the table so hard, it spilled. I got a towel and started wiping it up. As I did, his eyes locked on me, making me very uncomfortable. I kept thinking, "Please stop looking at me!"

At forty-seven years old, I didn't think I needed to be having anything to do with a seventeen-year-old. However, I made the mistake of saying to mutual friends, a young couple, Alice and Jim, who I had become very close to, "If he was eighteen, he would be in trouble." The woman, Alice, told him what I said, then, later that day, told me he had responded, "Why wait?" Though I have dated younger guys before, I felt he was way too young even for me.

Jim knew I was attracted to John (since he was a very good guitar player and extremely handsome), but because of his age, he also knew I really didn't want to have anything to do with him. Despite this, when John called a few days later, asking if he could come by my apartment, Jim asked me if it would be all right. I just shrugged and answered, "I guess."

By the time John arrived, the three of us were drinking beer and listening to music in my living room. He sat close to me—and my heart skipped a beat. As the evening grew late, Jim and Alice prepared to leave and were going to take John with them. But he had apparently fallen asleep, and we couldn't wake him. So they asked if he could stay that night, and they would come and get him in the morning. I told them he could, that I had an extra pillow and blanket he could use.

Well, by the time my friends had reached the main door to the apartment building, John was wide awake and talking to me. I believe he had this planned and had only faked being asleep. I offered him the blanket and pillow, but he just grabbed me and kissed me. Though I tried to remain distant from him, emotionally, I couldn't refuse his advance. We went into the bedroom and there spent the night together. This was the beginning of our relationship.

The next day, Jim and Alice picked John up, took him home, and then returned to my apartment building. Alice gave me John's cell phone number (at his request), and I called him. Though I was still unsure of whether I should be going with him, we made plans to get together later that day.

After about a week, my best friend, Jennifer, questioned me about this relationship. She didn't think I shouldn't be going with John because of our age difference. Other people said the same thing, and I began questioning it myself, even though I was happy being around him. I eventually decided it wasn't right. So I called him and told him what others were saying, and that I had decided it would be best if we didn't see each other anymore.

For the next few days, I felt sad and missed John terribly. Alice stopped by and told me, "I don't think there's anything wrong with what you have with him. Don't let other people take away your happiness just because they don't agree with it." That was all the encouragement I needed; I immediately called John and made plans to see him again.

As our relationship grew, he eventually moved into my apartment. He strayed once, and we broke up, but later, he came back to me. My feelings for him had grown into something I didn't really want. We spent the summer together, going to the creek during the day and partying with friends at night. I worked during the day and began to feel tired all the time. (Being "over the hill" takes its toll!) Eventually, I had to take a break from him just so I could get some sleep. Still, he would call and talk to me for a few minutes, telling me he missed me and wishing we could spend time together. I just needed some sleep!

John was kind and very attentive to my needs. He'd even ask if it bothered me when he spent time with his friends without me. I would assure him that it didn't. Ever sensitive to my feelings, if I was upset, he became upset. And as far as he was concerned, I could do no wrong. A few times, he was even willing to fight for me. At a party at a friend's house, he asked one of the guys who kept hitting me on the rear to stop. Another time, a guy told me that I couldn't keep a man because I was a "bitch," and John told him not to talk to me that way. He even stood up to George a few times when he, George, would harass me by calling my phone and saying horrible things to me. John would take the phone away from me and tell him to quit calling me. George gave my phone number to a strange man who insisted *I* gave it to him and called several times in one night. Then George called me the same night and just wanted to upset me by "pushing my buttons." We were still married, but I had a restraining order on him because of the harassing calls. I was not used to men defending me, but John did. He was another "good guy." I felt safe around him also.

Though Abigale disagreed with my decision to have a relationship with John, she eventually discovered how wonderful a person he actually was. At first, she and Jennifer would often tell me they didn't like me going with him. Despite this, I encourage John to have patience with her because she really was an awesome young lady. (Abigale was twenty-four, and John had just turned eighteen.) John hesitated to speak with Abigale because he knew her feelings about him. Then one day, she was having a tough time; she learned a close friend had died in a wreck. He talked with her about it, listened to her problems, and ended up helping her through it. That's when she realized what I saw in him: his ability to comfort and support those he cared about. This would start a friendship between the two of them.

Our relationship ended primarily because of all the opposition we both faced from friends and family who thought we shouldn't be going together. The mother of one of John's friends told his mother about our relationship and threatened me to "give me a good country ass whipping" (as if it was any of her business what someone else's son and I did). Even my best friend, Jennifer, tried to break us up despite telling me she hadn't realize how happy John made me until she overheard me talking and laughing with him on the phone. She expressed her disapproval by not letting him in her house. Her excuse was he became too rowdy when drinking. But I knew she let boy-friends in her house who were far more rowdy than John ever was. When John's mother realized what was going on, she told him she would file charges against me if he didn't stay away from me. But not only did he not stay away, he moved in with me again in the house I shared with two friends. He finally stopped coming around at the request of his mother. We are no longer friends.

What bothered me most about our situation was it seemed everyone was more worried about John and me than about themselves. Even after we broke up, people still ran John down by saying he told others how bad I was even while he was living with me or telling me how bad John was (not that I believed any of it). The only thing I took away from all this was: why can't people just mind their own business?

* * * * * * * *

All these men shared several common qualities. They all have a good heart and treated me with kindness and respect. They all brought laughter into my life through their music and their loving personalities. All but Ronnie were excellent musicians who bright-ened my life with their talents. And mostly, they've all given me many good memories. Every once in a while, I still think of these guys. To each of them, I say a heartfelt *thank you!* for making my life better!

CHAPTER SIXTEEN

✦✦✦   ✦✦✦   ✦✦✦   ✦✦✦

My Life Today

THE LORD HAS SO BLESSED my life now that it is difficult to know where to begin. Just waking up in the mornings is a blessing! A wise man once told me, "It's a good day if my name is not in the obituaries!" This is quite true. You can't bless others if you're in the grave, but alive and living your life with God's help and wisdom, you have the chance to improve yourself, mend old wounds, and help someone less fortunate. The Bible is truly the Word of God for the whole world, and if you follow the wisdom He has so graciously given us, your life too will change for the better.

I have learned to say "I'm sorry" to the ones I love. They are the most powerful words I have encountered. Healing comes from those words, healing for both sides, not just mine. It makes it easier for others to forgive, and humbling yourself creates in you a much kinder heart.

Please and *thank you* are also important words in relationships. It is much easier to give to or help someone who says them. George and I have learned and grown together in many ways, but these three small words have helped us to be thankful for each other. There is no resentment or hesitation about following through with a request. Whether it's as simple as bringing a glass of water or as complex as building a new staircase, we always say these words for any act of kindness. Knowing our actions are appreciated encourages us to want to do more.

I finally learned the lesson that totally trusting anyone but God will only bring disappointment. He, on the other hand, will always keep His promises. Nothing and nobody but God can be there with you watching over and protecting you all the time. People leave or fail us, and things can be lost, stolen, or broken, but our Creator is always there. Only He can love us perfectly. And His love is so powerful that it remains even when we mess up.

Throughout my life, I've often wondered why I was here. The Lord has answered that question—and it has become a burning desire that will not cease. He has shown me I am here to help others who have been hurt by sexual, verbal, and/or physical abuse, and has created in me a heart of extreme compassion for everyone who has suffered from it. You too have a purpose. God does not make mistakes. If you ask, He will reveal to you at the right time what that purpose is, no matter who you are, where you came from, or what you may or may not have done. With His help, you can achieve your destiny.

After learning that I had lived in the same house with a serial killer, I turned to the only solution I knew could help: my Creator God. Knowing what I did about Jesus, I did not hesitate to rely on whatever He told me, either through the Bible or through His Spirit. Nothing else by itself ever did any good. Psychiatrists are helpful, but they can take years to help us sift through all the pain and suffering. But a few minutes a day with Jesus did more to help me than anyone or anything else. (Plus, was a lot less expensive!) I am not totally free of my past yet; I still have bad days, and nightmares still occasionally occur, but both are starting to be far less frequent. My Heavenly Father has made the healing process easier.

I no longer consider myself a victim. The Bible says I'm an overcomer, and that's precisely how I see myself. I refuse to wallow in self-pity. Sharing my story gives me strength, along with the opportunity to hear another's story of what he or she lived through. I encourage anyone who has had abuse in your life to remember: your story hasn't ended. There is help and healing in a man I know, Jesus Christ. He can heal your heart and all the negative, destructive thoughts that whirl in your mind like a dark, damp fog, making it difficult for you to see. But the light of God's love can dispel the darkness and clear away the fog. The distrust you have for others will fade. The hatred you feel for yourself will cease. But only with Jesus. His way is the only way to true healing and peace.

My marriage to George continues to grow stronger. I rediscover his funny sense of humor (something that, as I said, is very important to me in a mate), and now thoroughly enjoy being around him. Once he learned what I went through in my childhood, he has become much more patient, kind, and loving with me. Where before the trial he couldn't understand why I acted the way I did, he now knows the reason. He even requires his friends to treat me with greater respect than what they had previously given me. Although I still find some of them rather irksome, I've learned to tolerate and even love some of them. It hasn't been easy, but I believe God puts people in our lives to act as "sandpaper," using them to smooth out our rough spots in order to learn to be better members of His kingdom.

I have kept in touch with some of the people I met in San Marcos, especial Commander Penny Dunn. She has been a wonderful help in my search for the truth and always answers any questions I e-mail her. I asked how she discovered the other three known victims of Willie. She told me, and I quote, "The other victims were identified by looking at similar murders committed in the Central Texas area and Camp Lejeune area of North Carolina during the time Jenkins lived nearby. Two murders that matched were originally attributed to Henry Lee Lucas who falsely confessed to hundreds of homicides across the USA. Once Jenkins was identified as the suspect in the murder of Courtney, and we saw his multiple convictions for violent sexual offenses, I knew there had to be other victims, including other murder victims. We just had to find the cases and the links to Jenkins. Little bits of multiple investigations were all tracked down, and some of those leads resulted in strong circumstantial evidence of Jenkins being involved in the murder of Sara, Lilly, and Nina. Unfortunately, the physical evidence from these cases has long since been destroyed by the investigating agencies in North Carolina and Texas." I am still amazed at how hard she has worked to find closure for these families. Knowing the truth, no matter how horrible, has continued to help in my healing.

My children have now become more important to me than ever before. Although I've always loved them, it's now easier for me to express that love. JJ has always been my "good child." Despite growing up without a permanent father figure, he has become the best father to his two boys. JJ is now thirty-five and married in 2008. He is an excellent provider and works hard, as does his wife, Angel. A wonderful mother, she also has a knack for interior design and has made their modern but comfortable home simply gorgeous. One wall of their house is a chalkboard where she writes beautiful and inspirational sayings that always encourage me and make me smile.

JJ has always been the most responsible out of my three children. His choices in the past have always been good, and now that he's married with his own family, he makes even better ones. His choosing Angel as his wife is prime example. Her family is very close, and they spend a lot of time together. This is good for JJ because our family hasn't always been close. He has truly become a great husband and father, and I'm very proud of him. He has turned out to be one of the greatest men I know.

As sometimes happens with daughters-in-law, Angel and I at first didn't see eye to eye. I, like most mothers, didn't feel like she was good enough for my perfect child. But gradually over the years, I have grown to love her as if she were one of my own children. Her kind heart and quick, humorous one-liners eventually softened my attitude toward her. She has also given me the best gifts of my life, my granny babies! Being a grandmother has changed my life for the better, with the little one's giving me joy by their laughter and cute sayings.

JJ had another son with another woman when he was nineteen. The relationship didn't last, and Justin now lives in Minnesota. JJ sent me a photograph of him when he was very young, and that's all I've seen of him in 1999. He is, of course, beautiful, and I would love to meet and spend time with him. Because Justin is my grandson, I'll always love him, even if that never happens. I don't believe he knows of me or anything about me. He is now seventeen.

When JJ called to tell me of Justin's upcoming birth, he started the conversation by asking me if I knew any good names. "For puppies?" I asked. "No," he answered, then told me I would soon be grandmother. A grandmother! I was only thirty-five at the time and not ready for this life-changing experience that proved to the world (and me) that I was getting older. "Grandma" seemed to be the ultimate old-age word. Friends actually had to talk me into seeing this event as a good thing. Eventually, I did become excited about Justin's arrival. Abigale and I lived in low-income housing at the time.

JJ's next child (his first with Angel, and my second grandson) I nicknamed Granny's Monkey. (I call him this because he, like his father, likes to climb.) Before he was born, JJ and Angel had asked me what I wanted him to call me. Without hesitation, I answered, "Granny." I cried tears of joy when Mickey came into the world.

Mickey is still young enough that he loves to have me around so we can play together. One of our favorite games is for me to tell him that all his kisses are Granny's. He then says no, that they're his and takes off. I then chase him around the house until I catch him and get all his kisses. This makes him laugh, and the sound fills my heart with joy. I'm convinced that Mickey is one of the smartest children on earth, surpassing even my own. He knew how to count to ten; some colors and the alphabet, at the age of two. JJ was also teaching him how to count in Spanish. Whenever he looks at me with his big blue eyes (that he gets from his beautiful mother), my heart melts. He has brought more happiness into my life than I could possibly have hoped for. (He made me realize why those with grandchildren are usually so devoted to them.)

Granny's Pumpkin became the nickname of Angel and JJ's second child and my youngest grandson. When they told me he was coming, I became excited—as well as a little impatient—at the thought of having another grandchild. While he was still in Angel's womb, before I left after a visit, I would lay my hand on Angel's stomach and tell the child inside I love him too.

Sam was born exactly one week after I testified in Texas, and I had been leery of leaving, knowing his birth could happen anytime. At first, I was afraid to hold him because he was so small, being a newborn. I had grown used to being around Mickey and, despite having had three children of my own, was concerned that I might now be too rough with him. When I told JJ how I felt about holding the baby, I pointed to Mickey and said, "That's more my size." The young boy, taking my statement literally, responded, "No, Granny, that's *my* size." I knew though that if I wanted to bond with Sam, I would have to get over my fear. It took a few times, but I eventually did become comfortable holding his tiny body.

Sam is very mellow. He smiles almost constantly; yet, there is still a sense of seriousness about him. Once when he was eight months old, he touched his small cupped hand on my cheek and stared into my eyes for what seemed to be about half a minute. (His eyes, like his brother's, are also a beautiful blue.) Amazed at his ability to concentrate on me for that long, I had the distinct feeling he was telling me he loved me. What an awesome experience! This child loves to be held and kissed and will sit quite still while in someone's arms or lap. Granny's Pumpkin is amazing. (I call him Pumpkin for his large round cheeks.)

My daughter, Abigale, the only girl in my family, is the sunflower of my life. I call her that because she loves sunflowers and brings sunshine into my day whenever I talk or spend time with her. She has always kept me straight with her loving but stern words, not hesitating to tell me whenever I blew it. Nobody else ever took on this responsibility. She and I have been very close throughout most of her life.

Her teenage years were the hardest for both of us. This seems to be the worst time for most mother-daughter relationships, but especially ours, with the mother suffering from buried traumas that she could not face. Even during the worst times though, Abigale was there for me. After leaving Peter in Minnesota, we were by ourselves and held each other up. She is now closer than a friend, always listens to what I have to say and knows me better than anyone else in the world.

Abigale's own life hasn't been easy. Her first long-term relationship, live in, became abusive. It hurt me to see her go through it. She had moved from Poplar Bluff to Springfield, Missouri (about three hundred miles away), so I didn't have much contact with her and didn't realize just how much she was hurting. After five years, she left her partner and came back to Poplar Bluff.

That's when I learned what she had endured: name-calling, occasional violence, being cheated on, and being blamed for everything that had gone wrong in the relationship. My heart went out to her because I could fully understand how she felt, having endured the same abuse many times. For over a year, her ex begged her to return, but Abigale remained strong and stayed in Poplar Bluff. I was very proud of her!

When she returned, she tried to stay with me. But because I was still in the parting stage of my life with drinking daily, I didn't give her the respect, peace, and quiet she needed in order to heal, something I shall forever regret. It only took a few days before she realized that it might be better to stay with her grandmother. After two or three months there, she moved in with her best friend, Josh, who had asked her to move in (as roommate only) because he was losing a roommate and needed the extra help.

I have come to love Josh as my own son, being willing to do anything for him that I could. He has helped Abigale heal from her abusive relationship. He has always been there to talk to her and give her advice and now they have become the best of friends, but not boyfriend/girlfriend. She has since moved out but visits Josh often. I love to be with them when they're together, not only because I love them but because they make a good comedy team, being silly and laughing almost nonstop whenever they're around each other. I'm inspired by seeing young people with such good hearts, especially a young man like Josh, thirty. He began calling me *boo*. I'm not sure why, and I now call him my boo bear. He's a wonderful part of our family, and everyone loves him!

JJ's wife, Angel, is a physical therapist, and Josh had become interested in this field. His starting college inspired Abigale to pursue a career in nursing. After being a certified nursing assistant for almost nine years, she took and passed the courses to be a licensed practical nurse. She now works full-time but still attends college to further her knowledge of nursing. Josh has bettered her life and continues to be her best friend. He is someone who encourages her by wanting her to succeed. A friend like that is irreplaceable; if you have one, hang on to them!

My youngest child, RJ, is once again a part of my life. Whenever I was separated from him, especially when he was younger, my heart always had an empty, hurting spot where he needed to be. When he came down for that first visit and I treated him so poorly, when he left, I feared I would never see him again. But when he came down for Thanksgiving in 2014, I was able to apologize and tell him how I felt, releasing that fear. He assured me that wouldn't happen. He doesn't speak with his father and feels like he belongs in our family. My healing process has made it easier for me to tell him I love him and to rest assured that he would not deliberately stay away just to hurt me. Though I have seen him only twice, he agrees with me that it would be nice to have the whole family together again now that I have a bit more sense.

When RJ was very young, he had been very affectionate and loved to snuggle, though he had a mean streak in him when it came to his sister, hitting her often (from a bit of sibling rivalry, no doubt). Losing him when he was only four years old, I missed out on most of his life. Though RJ is now in his twenties and over six feet tall, I would still like to treat him the child I lost. Unfortunately, I don't think he would fit in my lap. It's very painful to me when I think about the time I lost with him, but at least now, with the knowledge and perspective I've gained, we can restart our relationship and begin to make new memories. God does promise in His Word that He will restore the years that the cankerworm stole. Having RJ back in my life is only a small part of what my Heavenly Father has restored.

The family I have always hoped for is now in place. George's sister, Kerry, has become the sister I've always needed since I could no longer be with Brenda. I even call her my *baby sister*. She's very beautiful inside and out. She has dark hair with the most beautiful green eyes. She is a bit shorter than me, but not by much. This beauty contains a loving, kind, and helpful person who is always willing to listen. Along with her own two wonderful children, Kerry also takes care of her husband, Mark, and his five children, raising all of them as if they were her own and giving them the love they deserve. She is a true blessing in their lives as well as in mine.

George's parents are equally wonderful. His mother, whom I call Ma, is the best mother-in-law I've ever had. Giving, loving, smart, and beautiful, she has taken the time to get to know me well, yet still accepts me the way I am without criticism or condemnation. Ma also makes very warm and beautiful quilts and afghans, with the effort and love she puts into them being very apparent. We have several, and I will always cherish them. She also does several other crafts, crochet, embroidery, and they all come out gorgeous. Ma is very talented when it comes to making things with her hands.

My father-in-law has a wonderful sense of humor. Whenever Pa is around, he always makes me laugh. He too accepts me just the way I am. Pa is over seven feet tall while Ma is only about five feet tall, and they remind me of Ma and Pa Kettle and is the reason why I call them Ma and Pa. They both always tell me they love me, something that's very important for me to hear. I adore both of them!

Pa's immediate family has also become very important to me. Uncle Joe and Aunt Emily, who are now our neighbors, are wonderful people. We share food and help one another with whatever is needed, whenever it is needed, just like a real family. Uncle Joe visited George one day during the summer of 2014 and asked if we would be interested in moving into the small cabin on the Current River next to the family's large cabin. Well, when he mentioned it to me, I immediately said yes! Especially since Uncle Joe had also said if we didn't take the cabin, the family was going to burn it down.

The cabin has a lot of history. The original rock part that is now our bedroom was built in the 1930s, along with several others on the property that used to be the city park. In the '50s, those cabins that weren't owned by individuals were rented to people who came for the river. Most of the cabins have been torn down to build houses on the properties, except ours and two other still on Ma and Pa's lot. Our cabin had been added to on the side and top, making it somewhat of a two-story split level. Seeing how tiny the original buildings were make me appreciate our cabin even more.

After agreeing to take this piece of Ripley County history, the first day I walked into it, I could tell I had my work cut out for me. It was literally a disaster. Five dogs had been kept in the building—two males and three females—and none of them had been let out to do their "business." Consequently, the place was full of feces and urine, and the smell almost knocked me over. All I could say was, "Wow!"

George and I tackled the mess, taking three long months to clean it enough to move in during the month of October. Uncle Joe and George replaced part of the kitchen subfloor and put new flooring down in the kitchen, bathroom, and living room. Just doing this made the house look new. In addition to helping, Uncle Joe also paid for all the flooring. This is only part of all that he had done for us, and I'll be forever thankful.

The rest of the remodeling has been slow with much that still needs to be done, but at least now it looks and smells more like a house. We consider our cabin another rescue since the family were just going to burn it down. No one wanted the task of cleaning it, but we took it on because we saw the beauty of the place. And it is indeed now our beautiful home.

Living in that cabin on the Current River has been a true blessing, especially being able to wake up every morning to the sights and sounds of the natural beauty of the place. The river is in sight on the northwest side of the house, always flowing dark green. Watching the water swiftly going by is soothing to my soul.

Along with the river and trees are several types of birds that visit our yard. Woodpeckers, finches, robins, hummingbirds, and mourning doves all come through our property to find food, make nests, or just stop to rest. Once a turkey vulture even landed in our yard. I couldn't believe how big he was, as large as a four or five-year-old child. My favorite bird, though, is the beautiful bald eagle that flies up and down the river in warmer weather. It is an amazing sight to see him soaring gracefully on his powerful wings.

The very first time I met Uncle Joe's wife, Emily, I fell in love with her. She treated me kindly, has a humorous streak that always makes me laugh, and, like her husband, and is very giving. She has surprised me with several nice gifts: two wreaths for me to put flowers in and a nice picture of a sunflower to decorate my kitchen. I'm very thankful to have them as my neighbors.

I often tell George that he's my superhero: he has rescued our two dogs, our house, and me. Without him, none of us would be where we are today. That's the kindness of my husband's heart. My Heavenly Father has blessed me with a wonderful man!

I am slowly learning to forgive myself. I still have guilt and shame for the way I have treated some people. My desire is to make the lives of those around me better, so I need to be the best I can be. Turning my "I can't" into "I can!" has helped me, as well as knowing my life is not a waste and that God has had a perfect plan for me from the start. Don't ever say you can't; that is the worst enemy of your healing and improving your life. You can! Take baby steps, figure out what works for you, and always include God in your life. He knows you better than you even know yourself, and His counsel will always be the best. He created you, so He knows every one of your secrets and imperfections and will gladly give you the strength you need to overcome any obstacles in your life.

As for my siblings, I'm grateful that Brenda and I are communicating again, though not as often as I'd like. The relationship with my brothers, however, has remained pretty much the same. We still are not as close I'd like to be, but I do talk to them. I'm not sure how they feel about all of the pain or the lies Joan has brought into our family or if they believe what happened. I sent them a copy of the article from the local paper about my speaking before the child advocacy group to let them know I am doing something good with my life. I have always been the black sheep of our family with the lifestyle I chose and not finishing college. I do miss my brothers and would love to have a great relationship with them. But they never experienced the mother that I did—Joan was always a good mother to them—so I don't even know if they could understand how I feel about her.

I still find it extremely difficult to forgive Joan. If what she did had only affected me, then maybe it wouldn't be so hard. But she knew what Willie was doing, and to not say anything to anyone, allowing him to continue raping and killing women and refusing to give information that could have helped authorities solve the crimes he had already committed, is hard to overlook. Though I don't wish any harm to her, I cannot keep her as part of my life. I cannot even think of her as my mother. She continues even now to lie to and hurt me, and that is not something I want or need in my life right now. I'm on a journey of healing, so I must stay away from those who caused the pain in the first place. I only pray that someday it will be different.

Joan and Willie's daughter, Izzy, is also no longer part of my life. My stepsister believes her mother, believes that I'm the one who is lying. Someday, though, I hope she wakes up, takes a closer look at everything and everyone, and realizes the truth. If that day comes, Joan will find herself reaping what she has sown.

I have forgiven Willie, though. I know he will reap what he has sown: the death penalty. I didn't want to hold on to the hatred I had for him, so I released it in the courtroom when I stood up to him and told the truth. Sometimes I even feel sorry for him. I wouldn't want to be someone who, by the choices I made, destroy every life I came in contact with or who hindered—and even stopped—others from being the best they can be, altering those lives forever for the worst. My only hope for him is that he will find the love and salvation of Jesus before he is executed.

I end with a little advice for my brothers and sisters in the Lord. Brothers, be careful how you treat your sisters. You never know what they've been through, or the secrets some of us hide. Sisters, have respect for yourselves. Hold your head up and walk through life like true daughters of the Most High! Be kind and forgiving to others, especially in your own households. Make your home as peaceful and loving as you possibly can no matter what happens.

I sincerely hope that those reading this book will find at least some of the answers you seek. I want only to make life better for those who are hurting, if only by letting you know you are not alone. There is an end to your suffering, and there is help. Don't ever give up. Keep fighting for yourself and others, and always, always, always rely on Jesus. He is the *only* way to *true and complete healing*!

POSTSCRIPT

As MY EDITOR AND I were working on finalizing my book and getting it ready to send to the publisher, my world was shattered. George, the husband whom I thought would finally be the one I would spend the rest of my life with, gave me what has to be the worst Christmas present I have ever received.

At 7:30 p.m. on Christmas Day 2016, after supposedly spending the day hunting with friends, George came home and told me he was in love with another woman and wanted to be with her. He quickly added that he loved me too and would let me stay at the cabin while he paid all the bills, but the damage had already been done. My whole world fell apart at that moment. I was blindsided and didn't see any of this coming. This man, whom I had lived with and loved for three and a half years, whom I had stood up for so others wouldn't take advantage of him, all while working hard to make us a beautiful home, didn't want me anymore. I was devastated.

Before he left to spend that night with Candy (the other woman), he claimed to have told me two weeks before that he was done with me. If he did, I didn't—and still don't—remember. After calling a friend and crying on her shoulder over the phone, I spent a lonely, sleepless night. The next day, December 26, 2016, I left that home and George behind and haven't been back since. On March 20, 2017, I filed for divorce, only waiting that long because of my limited income.

What made my pain even worse was the fact that the woman George left me for *had* been a good friend. I had fond memories of George and I going to Candy and her husband's house in the summer to swim and spend time on the river. But then, on November 3, 2016, she shot her husband to death, claiming self-defense. That made both George and I feel sorry for her and tried to help her any way we could. But as time passed, and then George left me to be with her, I began to wonder about the truthfulness of her claim. Her words and actions just didn't seem like those of a grieving widow.

I guess I'm just an eternal optimist, seeing and believing only the best from those I put my trust in because I should have seen this coming when I found two text messages from Candy shortly before George left. After reading them, I began to wonder what was going on between my husband and my "friend" since both messages had sexual undertones. Five days later, I found out. (According to the phone records that I went through after I moved out, I discovered they had been repeatedly texting each other since December 7!)

While living at the office, I started doing Internet research on George's behavior. It matched the definition of a narcissist perfectly. This is a person who has an overexaggerated view of self-worth. Simply put, they think too much of themselves, and others are easily disposed of when the abuser is done with them since the other person no longer has any value to them.

Before all this happened, I didn't know this personality disorder existed. As I have educated myself about it, all the symptoms were there, screaming at me from the pages. Narcissists are arrogant, manipulative, two-faced pathological liars who use others for their own gain, often by putting those others down to make themselves look good. They are impatient, angry, and unable to take criticism. Seeking constant praise for themselves, they are unable to fulfill the needs of others.

Thinking of our life together, I now see that George had exhibited every one of these behaviors. (And the woman he's now with does too! It should be interesting to see what happens between them.) I now can understand why he was so quick to go with me for Willie Jenkins's sentencing trial and why, as I struggled with my PTSD, he was willing to stay and help me. It fed his ego and made him look good. But when I no longer needed him in that way, he no longer needed me.

I am grateful for the time I had with George—grateful he was with me at Willie's trial and grateful that he stayed with me as long as he did. But he has made his choice, and now I've made mine.

I'm thankful the Lord took me out of that situation and has given me the necessary healing that goes along with it. Knowing the truth about George's relationship with Candy has helped that healing to continue every day. I have found a wonderful group of women in a closed group on Facebook (this means no one else can see our post but members, so I feel safe there). It is a small group of five hundred women from everywhere! Some from England, several states, and across the globe. These women understand me, and like me, some have even been in relationships with a narcissist. Most have been left for another woman or cheated on. Being able to relate to others going through the same situations has helped me to understand why George is like he is. I'm realizing he has always treated me like I was his third or fourth priority, never first.

These women and I laugh together, support one another, cry, share our heartaches, our accomplishments, and encourage one another. There is a young lady named April from Colorado whom I have become close with. She has helped me through some of my roughest days, and I always end up smiling after talking with her. These women have become a life source to me, and I appreciate all of them.

Since leaving George, I have become reclusive. I stay in the back of my office, locking the doors after hours and seldom going out. I have lived here for a little over six months. The only items I have with me are those I took out of the house the day I left: clothes, a few pictures, two blankets and pillows, my coffeepot, and of course, my Bible. Friends loaned me other items that have helped to make my stay in the office more comfortable. I only wish I could have brought my dogs as well since I miss them terribly.

My healing is coming together, and each day, I'm thankful for what I do have. I hope to be moving into an apartment as soon as my finances allow it (car repairs and lawyer and publisher fees have so far taken up most of my income). God has protected me, loved me through the pain, and healed my heart. I'm forever grateful to Him.

I don't see what happened between me and George as an end. Instead, I see it as the beginning of a new and better life. I only hope that those reading this book will find at least some of the answers you seek. I want only to make life better for those who are hurting, if only by letting you know you are not alone. There is an end to your suffering, and there is help. Don't ever give up. Keep fighting for yourself and others, and always rely on Jesus. He is the way to *true and complete healing*!

ABOUT THE AUTHOR

KAREN WOODS LIVES IN A small rural community in southeast Missouri. She has three children and three grandchildren. This is her first publication.

CPSIA information can be obtained
at www.ICGtesting.com
Printed in the USA
LVHW07s1002150718
583819LV00039B/255/P